METASTOCK® in a NUTSHELL

SIMON SHERWOOD

D1615554

MetaStock software and the MetaStock name used by permission and courtesy of Equis International. All charts in this book were created using MetaStock.

Published by John Wiley & Sons, Inc., Hoboken, New Jersey

First published in Australia by Wrightbooks,
an imprint of John Wiley & Sons Australia, Ltd

For general information on our other products and services, or technical support, please contact our Customer Care Department within the United States at 800-762-2974, outside the United States at 317-572-3993 or fax 317-572-4002.

Wiley also publishes its books in a variety of electronic formats. Some content that appears in print may not be available in electronic books.

For more information about Wiley products, visit our web site at www.wiley.com.

ISBN 0 701637 39 0

Printed in Australia by McPherson's Printing Group.

10 9 8 7 6 5 4 3 2 1

Contents

Contents (Cont'd)

*To my parents Joan and Arthur –
thank you for giving me such a great start to life.*

Acknowledgments

This book would not have been possible without the support and encouragement of my friends, work associates and the EI MUG (Educated Investor MetaStock User Group) members.

In particular I would like to thank Janene Murdoch (Educated Investor Bookshop), Alan Hull (ActVest), Ryan Eborn, Alice Feld and Dan Smith (Equis International) for their belief in me.

I am also very grateful for the guidance and input from the following people whom I have been fortunate to have dealings with:
Daryl Guppy, Louise Bedford and Chris Tate.

Last and certainly not least, to Sharyn my soul mate, thank you for your unconditional support – and, I'm back… well, until I start the next one!

MetaStock is a product of Equis International

Achelis Binary Wave, DataOnDemand, The DownLoader, Expert Advisor, The Explorer, Visual Control, QuoteCenter, MetaStock Performance Systems, and Smart Charts are trademarks of Equis International. Equis, MetaStock, and OptionScope are registered trademarks of Equis International. Reuters is a registered trademark of Reuters Limited. Signal is a registered trademark of Data Broadcasting Corporation. IBM is a registered trademark of International Business Machines Corporation. MS-DOS, Microsoft Windows, Microsoft Windows 95, Microsoft Windows 98, Microsoft Windows NT, Microsoft IntelliMouse, Microsoft Office, Microsoft Word, Microsoft Excel, and Paint are registered trademarks of Microsoft Corporation. ODDS is a trademark of Fishback Management & Research Co. All other product names or services mentioned are trademarks or registered trademarks of their respective owners.

The MetaStock product is not a recommendation to buy or sell, but rather a guideline to interpreting the specified analysis methods. This information should only be used by investors who are aware of the risk inherent in securities trading. Equis International and Trading Systems Analysis Group accept no liability whatsoever for any loss arising from any use of this product or its contents.

Introduction – or Read Me First!

Version 8

MetaStock Version 8 is now available. Images relevant only to Version 8 will be shown in a box like this.

 Phew... here it is—after many hours of work and enjoyment (and only a tiny little amount of frustration), *MetaStock® in a Nutshell* has finally seen the light of day.

MetaStock certainly needs little by way of introduction. Even if you had not heard of it before, by the time you have purchased the product, chances are you have found out not only how powerful it is but also that it is one of the most popular charting packages in the world.

Here are what some of its fans like about MetaStock:

➤ Its intuitive drag-and-drop charting tools, which speed up the learning process.

➤ It is suitable for both beginners and more advanced users.

➤ There are over 120 built-in indicators to help you analyze the markets— you can place them on a chart with a simple drag-and-drop action.

➤ The ability to customize the built-in indicators that MetaStock already has, or build your own with the Indicator Builder.

➤ There are nine styles of clear and crisp charts for you to look at.

1

➤   Its layouts, templates and more—you are able to apply favorite indicators, time periods, colors and other settings to create templates which you can save and overlay on your charts.

➤   You can create a layout of stocks which you can open and view at the same time—with just one click of the mouse.

➤   There is complete documentation, both in print and online, for easy help when you need it.

➤   There is the facility to drag and drop an item within a chart into another chart, or into another program like Excel or Word.

See www.MetaStock.com for more information.

MetaStock Awards

The fact that it has been awarded the following prizes also speaks volumes about its popularity.

Technical Analysis of Stocks & Commodities Reader's Choice Awards:

MetaStock: Trading Software $US200 – $US499
Winner: 2001, 2000, 1999, 1998, 1997, 1996, 1995, 1994, 1993.

Futures Magazine Four-Disk Award (highest rating given):

MetaStock
Winner: January 1997, August 1995.

Well, enough about MetaStock for now. I think you have the idea, no further introduction required.

This *Nutshell* book, on the other hand, probably does need some introducing. Now hopefully you are still with me and haven't decided to skip the 'boring' Introduction to get to the good stuff. This is not just any Introduction, this is where I will let you know some very IMPORTANT things that you NEED to know, before you try and work through this book. Take the time to read this and make sure you have the required 'Windows' knowledge and your MetaStock charting journey will all be smooth sailing.

Learning to use a new piece of software is always a challenge. This task can be made increasingly difficult if you, the reader, do not have any knowledge of the wonderful world of Windows. If you are still thinking that Windows are only for looking through then I STRONGLY suggest you get yourself along to the educational body in your area and do some basic computer courses that cover Windows. Knowing the basics of how to use a computer with Windows 95, 98,

2000, ME or whatever other version of Windows you have will make your learning of this new piece of software much more enjoyable.

So, from this point on, I am assuming that you are familiar with how to use Windows. This means you know how to (at the very least):

➤ Access drop down menus.

➤ Select files.

➤ Select multiple files.

➤ Right and left click the mouse—including the 'double click'.

➤ Maximize and minimize windows.

➤ Find files.

➤ Launch programs.

➤ Load software.

➤ Create and delete directories.

➤ Play solitaire and mine sweeper (!)

➤ Do all the other fun things that the Windows operating system lets you do.

Should you decide to proceed without any Windows knowledge, then I think your journey will be tough, very tough, much tougher than you could imagine. It will be like driving down a dirt road with four flat tyres—not much fun, very uncomfortable and oh so very, very frustrating!

It would also be extremely useful if you had some prior knowledge of technical analysis and charting. Again, if this isn't the case, it may be best to read up on the subject or attend one of the many and varied courses on the subject.

Now we've got that sorted out, I can tell you what this book is really all about. It has been written as a guide for the brand new MetaStock user. Yep! The people who have bought the box, installed the program on their computers and are now sitting looking at the screen wondering, "What the heck do I do with it now, and *how* do I do it?" Well, at last we have a guide for beginners on how to use this great piece of software.

Get comfortable at your computer, open this book, start the program and turn the pages when you hear the bell—if you don't hear the bell, just pretend. *MetaStock® in a Nutshell* will cover the basics to get you up and analyzing your charts as quickly and painlessly as possible. By working through this book you will learn how to use many of the basic features of MetaStock. However, due to the power and complexities of MetaStock, some of the more advanced features have been left out; maybe they will appear in the next one (send all requests for a future title, 'Advanced MetaStock® in a Nutshell', to the publisher!).

I have listed below some of the things that you will be doing by the end of this book. Note that not only will you be doing these things, you will be doing them with considerable ease (due to the power of MetaStock and this book, of course):

➤   Opening charts and annotating them as required.

➤   Plotting and building indicators.

➤   Creating multi-chart layouts.

➤   Making and using new templates.

➤   Exploring and filtering stocks.

One last thing before we get to the fun stuff, I just want to confirm what this book will not do. *MetaStock® in a Nutshell* will NOT:

➤   Teach you how to trade.

➤   Make any 'buy' or 'sell' recommendations.

➤   Teach you technical analysis.

There are lots of great trading and technical analysis books available. I have listed a selection of them in the 'Further Reading' section. They range from the classics to modern day best-sellers—there really are some fantastic books available.

Now we know what it won't do, we also know what this book WILL do and that is give you a solid foundation on using the world's most popular charting software.

A final last word, this is by no means a definitive book on MetaStock. Nor are the methods contained herein the only way to do things in MetaStock. MetaStock is a very powerful program and like any Windows program, things can be done in several ways. Each user will find his or her own way to do things—in this book are some of the methods that I have found to work and are used by people who rely on the software to make their investment decisions.

OK... let's get into it!

1

Some Basics to Get You Started

 **IN A NUTSHELL** WE WILL COVER:

A bit about formats and definitions.

Launching the software and getting past the 'warm up' screen.

The different parts of the screen (in readiness for Chapter 2).

A note about some other MetaStock tools.

Accessing data and Load Options.

How to get help.

Read this first and learn the basic tools and terminology you need to get you through the rest of the book.

We are going to start by covering a few very basic things about using MetaStock and some of the components that are built into the software to help you on your way.

Once you have loaded MetaStock, completed the registration card and organized your data, you are ready to begin your journey.

Format Used

Just a note on the way things are formatted in this book. Any time an onscreen button or drop down menu is referenced, it is shown in quotation marks with the hot key marked with an underscore (as it appears on the screen). For example, if I refer to the File drop down menu, it will appear as 'File', and so on. Buttons will be shown in the same way, like the Help button, which would appear like this: 'Help'. When I refer to dialog boxes, they will be similarly displayed, for example: the 'Open Chart' dialog box.

Also, in most of the dialog boxes (where there is a choice!) you will note that I have used the 'Details' type view. This is from the 'Open Chart' dialog box and shows my current view…so to speak!

Some Terms Used

During the course of this book, I will use the terms 'stock' or 'security' when talking about whatever it is we are plotting… or talking about! For the purpose of this book, I will consider these terms interchangeable.

Data is the stuff we will plot or chart in MetaStock. It can be stock prices, futures, indexes, commodities or any other 'thing' you want to study.

Launching MetaStock

Let's get into it now and launch the program. (You will know how to do this, because you know how to use Windows!)

When you launch the program for the very first time, after a few anxious pauses you will see the following screen:

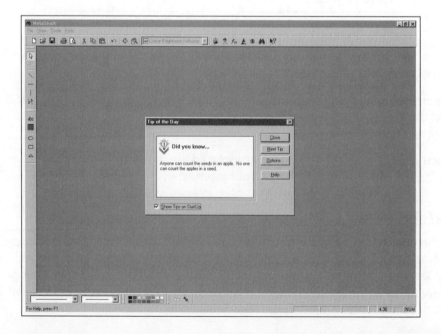

Like many Windows programs, MetaStock provides you with a 'Tip of the Day'. It's worth leaving this feature on as you may find the tips to be very useful and with a program like MetaStock, you can never have too much knowledge. The type of Tips can even be customized (using the 'Options…' button) to be more appropriate to your level, from beginner to advanced, and include a few 'other' types of tips—just for fun (see the previous example).

For now, close this window so we can get through all the basic stuff as quickly as possible. (Chapter 2 is where the real fun starts, or is that Chapter 3!?) You will then see the following window:

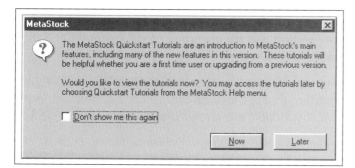

You can choose to do these Tutorials now or access them later. My suggestion… come back to them later! If you leave the tick box blank next to 'Don't show me this again', then you will have the option to run the MetaStock Quickstart Tutorials each time you start MetaStock. If you don't like that option, then tick the box and come back to them any time via the 'Help' drop down menu.

Now you should be looking at the following screen… wondering what to do next and hoping the next chapter is going to be more exciting. (It will be, trust me!)

However, there is a chance that you may not have got to this point, which could be due to any or all of the following reasons:

1. The software is not installed correctly.

2. The software is not installed at all.

3. You get some funny message about Reuters DataLink and Internet access.

4. Something else!

If you are not using Reuters DataLink, then make sure that both the User ID and password in the Reuters DataLink tab (you can check this via the 'Tools' drop down menu and then selecting 'Options…') are both blank. Otherwise, each time you launch Metastock, the program will try to connect to the Internet and then connect to the Reuters DataLink site.

For any other problems with getting to this point, either try installing the software again, check the documentation that comes with the package or seek help from your software supplier. Most suppliers are knowledgable enough to help you get up and running.

What's on the Screen?

Let's have a look at a standard MetaStock screen and see what's actually on it.

I've jumped the gun a bit here as at this stage you probably don't know how to create this screen. Never mind, it is just to show you the different parts so you know what they are when we talk about them later.

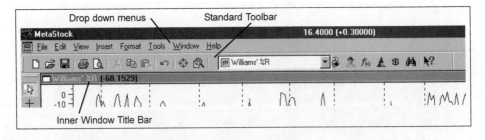

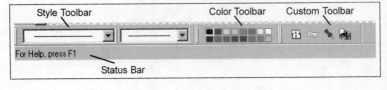

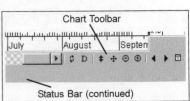

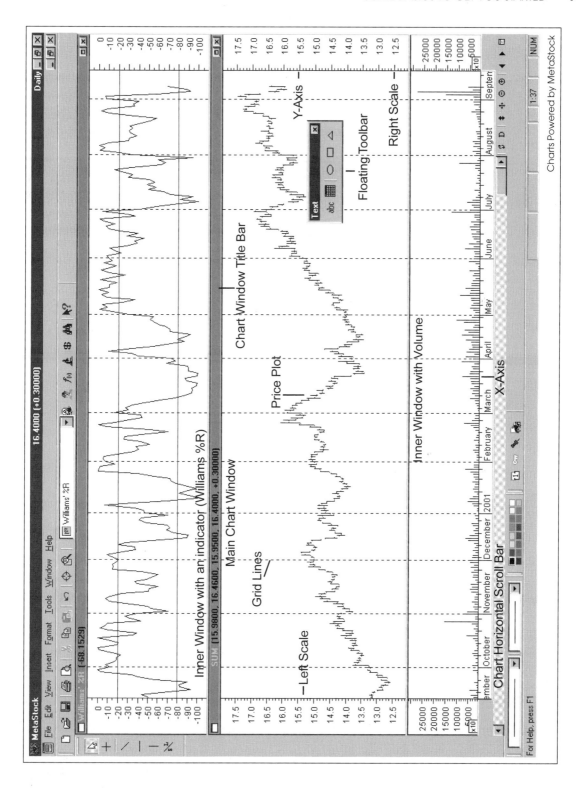

So you see, there is lots on the screen. Some of it will even be familiar to you because it is standard Windows speak, i.e. drop down menus and toolbars.

Later on, once you are more familiar with the product, you will be able to customize the screen to suit your own style—for example, where you have the scales, what values show in the title bars, the colors used and if you want the grid lines to show, to name but a few.

You can decide what toolbars you want by accessing the 'Toolbars' menu from the 'View' drop down menu. From the menu, pick and choose the toolbars you want. They can be 'docked' or 'floating' as in other Windows-based programs. For now, leave the toolbars as they are. However, do remember that if one goes missing for some strange reason (no questions asked), you can retrieve it by reselecting it in the 'Toolbars' menu.

Where it is and What it Does

Besides the many charting tools that MetaStock has, there are some other tools that are well worth mentioning. Some of these will be covered in this book, others won't be covered until another day.

From left to right the icons are (and briefly what they do):

The Downloader:	Used to manipulate data and download data from a compatible data supplier.
*Expert Advisor:	Also known as the 'Charlie Chaplin' icon. A collection of powerful tools to automate your technical analysis.
*Indicator Builder:	This is what you use to build your own indicators using the powerful MetaStock Formula language.
Optionscope:	For analyzing options on futures and equities.
*System Tester:	Used to back-test and analyze trading systems.

Explorer:	Used to search and rank securities according to particular criteria, e.g. find all stocks for which today's closing price was greater than yesterday's closing price, or for which the closing price was greater than a specified Moving Average.

(*The MetaStock Formula Language is common across these tools.)

These tools can also be accessed via the 'Tools' drop down menu and each have keyboard shortcuts.

The Downloader, Expert Advisor, Optionscope and System Tester will not be covered in this book. However, Chapter 10 will include:

➤ A small Expert you can create to change the color of your candlestick charts

➤ A quick look at the Maximum Profit System (in the System Tester)—great to impress your friends!

We will use the Indicator Builder in Chapter 4 and the Explorer will be 'explored' in Chapter 9.

Accessing Your Data

The only thing now remaining before we really get started is to make sure we can read the data. It doesn't matter where or how you get your data, as long as you know where it is stored on your computer. When you know its whereabouts, you simply point MetaStock to that directory.

To load a chart, we use either the 'New' or 'Open' options (these will be explained in the next chapter). For now, access these via the 'File' drop down menu, then select 'New' and then 'Chart…'. This brings up the security selection screen; from here we must lead MetaStock to the correct data directory.

Click the large 'Local Data' icon (the middle icon on the left-hand side) and, using the drop down 'Look in:' box and the available folders, navigate to the correct data directory.

It is then a matter of selecting the appropriate directory to access the required stock or index.

You can start off by installing the data that was packaged with MetaStock. Simply follow the instructions that came with the MetaStock end-of-day data CD. Then to access this with MetaStock we use the drop down menu to navigate to and select the directory as we would in Windows Explorer. The screen would look something like the image overleaf.

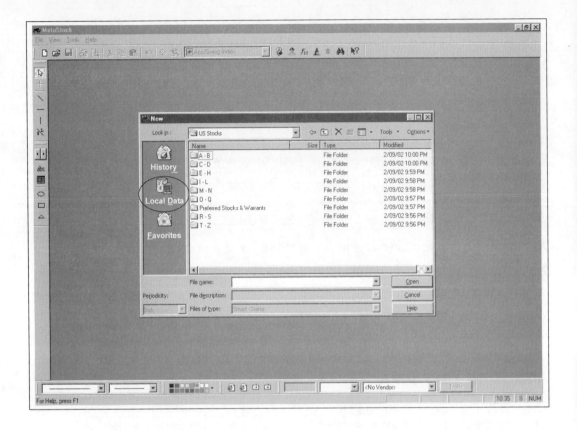

Load Options

Another thing to look at is the 'Load Options…' in the 'Options' drop down menu (in the 'New' or 'Open File' dialog box).

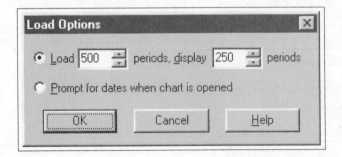

This allows you to control how much data is loaded in and how much is displayed. By default (when you first load MetaStock), the number of periods loaded is set to 500 (approximately two years worth). This means the program will load 500 trading periods and display 250 of them.

For now, I would suggest changing the figure to 5,000, to give you more data to play with. Otherwise it looks like you only have about two years of data, when in fact most of the time you will have considerably more (although it does depend on the history available for the particular stock). The other option is to have MetaStock prompt you for the dates each time you open a chart. There are certainly times where this can be useful, but for now, we'll just stick with the '5,000' periods.

HELP!

OK, this is definitely the last part of the 'basics'. It is just as important as all the other tools, so please don't gloss over it.

MetaStock, like all quality Windows-based programs, has great built-in support. We have already seen things like the 'Tip of the Day' function and the Tutorials, but it doesn't stop there.

Help is available in the following ways:

1. Selecting 'Help' from the drop down menu.

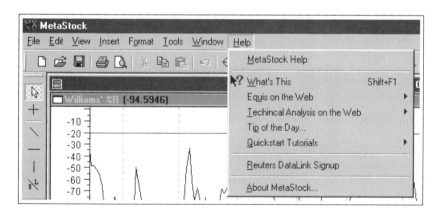

2. Selecting a 'Help' button from within a dialog box (like in the 'Open' dialog box).

3. Hitting 'F1' on the keyboard—for context-sensitive help.

4.   Using the [?] button on the Standard Toolbar and clicking on something you want to know about.

Just about everything in the printed manual is available on your computer through the program Help options. It should also be noted that the Help system is consistent with 'normal' Windows Help screens.

There, the basics are over! In the next chapter we will actually open a chart and start doing things to it. You can proceed past this point if you have got the software up and running and have found the data directory. If not, please re-read this chapter and seek assistance where required. Again, your software supplier may be able to help, as may your data provider.

Version 8

Here is a summary of the new features offered in Version 8:

➤   Enhanced System Tester with multiple securities and systems testing, online data testing, enhanced customization and analysis reports

➤   Online Explorations...no need to download

➤   Eight new volume-based Explorations

➤   Equidistant Channel Line Study

➤   Windows Color Palette...custom colors for line studies, indicators, price styles, etc.

➤   Download up to 6,000 securities per folder.

2

Now...
On to Doing Things!

 **IN A NUTSHELL** we will cover:

Smart Charts and not so smart Charts.

Restoring Smart Charts — if the Computer 'messes' them up.

Changing the style of Chart.

Changing the way the screen looks.

Changing the scales.

The Chart Toolbar — the time period, zooming and scrolling.

Drawing on the Chart — trendlines, support and resistance lines, text and smiley faces, which are commonly referred to as, er... symbols.

Learning how to use MetaStock is a bit like learning to walk, you do it step by step.

Here is the start of another step on your MetaStock journey—time to cover some more practical 'doing' things.

Smart Charts

The first thing we have to understand is the difference between Smart Charts and not so smart Charts... commonly referred to as Charts!

When we use MetaStock, we can either create a new Chart from our data or open an existing Smart Chart or a Chart we have previously saved. If this is your first time using the program or you have never saved a Chart, then you will only be able to open a Smart Chart or create a new Chart.

So what is a Smart Chart? Well, it's a semi-intelligent chart that automatically saves any changes you make to it, like adding a trendline, Moving Average, or if you decide to change the style of the chart from, say, a bar chart to a candlestick chart. Any changes you make to regular Charts, on the other hand, must be saved or they will not show up next time you open that particular Chart. When you close a Chart, you will be prompted to save the changes. You are never prompted with a Smart Chart, because it saves the changes as soon as you do them—what a smart little chart!! Probably the best way to understand what this means is to open a Smart Chart (of which you will see there are already default ones in MetaStock) and then create a Chart to see all this in action.

Opening a Smart Chart

To open a Smart Chart we can use either:

1. The 'Open' icon on the Standard Toolbar; or

2. The 'File' drop down menu to access 'Open...'.

I guess it comes down to personal preference how you do it, as with most Windows-type programs there is usually more than one way to access a particular feature. There is even a keyboard shortcut ('Ctrl+O') too!

Whatever method you choose will then take you to the 'Open' dialog box (shown at the top of the next page).

From here, select a file to open—note that 'Smart Charts' should be showing in the 'Files of type:' drop down box and the 'Local Data' button should be pushed in.

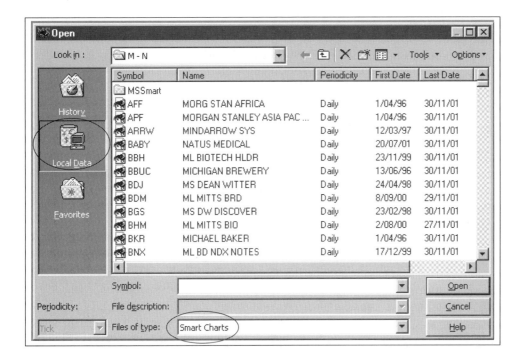

Pick a stock, any stock; for now it's not important. I've selected Microsoft, so the screen for me now looks like this:

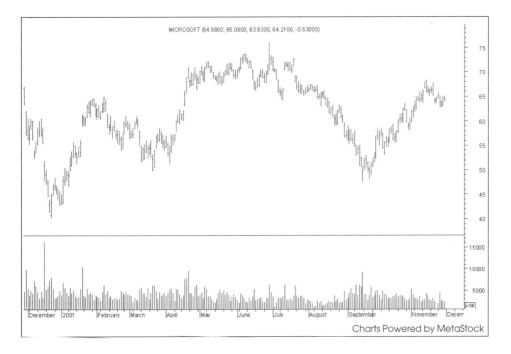

Trendlines

Let's add a trendline to our Microsoft Smart Chart.

Just before we do this, a quick word on trendlines. There is much debate about the hows, wheres and whys of trendlines and I am not going to add any fuel to that. Needless to say, there is some consensus that they are a useful tool if used as part of an overall trading or investing strategy.

OK, now we are going to draw a trendline on our chart. How you place it, of course, will depend on your own rules for drawing trendlines (of which there are many!). Select the 'Trendline' tool by clicking on the diagonal line icon on the Trendline toolbar.

Move the cursor to the chart and notice how the cursor now shows as a pencil. You can draw on the chart by clicking and dragging the line whilst holding the left mouse button down. Release the left button to end the line—voilá! One trendline.

Like most things in MetaStock, trendlines are objects that can be moved or altered once drawn on the chart. Move the pointer or mouse over the line and see the pointer change. If you click the mouse (left click), then the trendline is selected and any changes will affect the trendline object. You can move the pointer to the extreme ends of the Trendline (when it is selected, squares—called 'handles'—will show at the ends of the line); the pointer now has a 'hand' on it, meaning you can drag or move that particular point. This is useful for altering the position of a trendline. All this will become clearer when you actually do it, so try these things out later and see what happens.

Now back to our chart. What you are looking at might look something like the chart on the opposite page.

Where you draw the line is not important, the main thing is to put a line of some sort on the chart.

Now let's test this out... close the chart—using whatever method suits your style best. I like using the cross in the upper right corner (which is fine as long as you don't hit the wrong one and close MetaStock down!).

OK, so what happened? Well, MetaStock closed the Smart Chart and there was no prompt to save the change you had made. I guess the only way to really test this out is to open the Smart Chart again and hope it really was smart. Try that now. Are you sitting there amazed? If so, you are probably looking at the Smart Chart complete with the change you made, i.e. your trendline is still there.

This is how Smart Charts work. We can make any changes to a Smart Chart, like drawing on trendlines, and it will automatically save the changes.

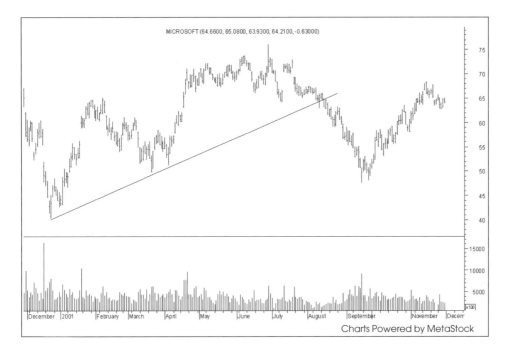

MICROSOFT (64.6600, 65.0800, 63.9300, 64.2100, -0.63000)

Charts Powered by MetaStock

Now we'll compare it to a Chart.

Creating a Chart

Before we can open a Chart, we have to create one. To do this we select 'Ne̲w' either using:

1. The 'New Chart/Layout' icon on the Standard Toolbar; or

2. The 'F̲ile' drop down menu.

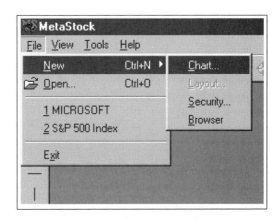

This will bring up the 'New' dialog box from which we can select a share (see over the page).

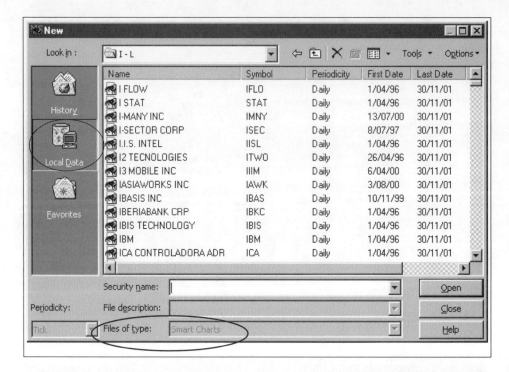

Note that the 'Files of type:' box is grayed out so that we can't access its drop down box—what we are doing is creating a brand new Chart from our data.

OK, I chose IBM, so here is my Chart:

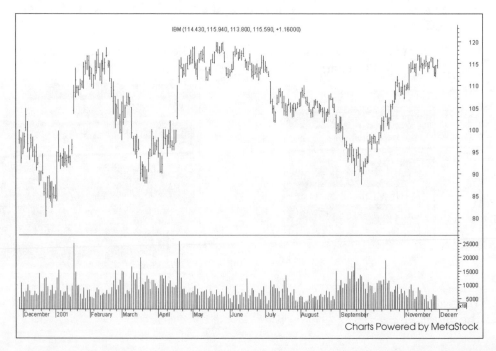

Now let's do exactly what we did before and draw a trendline on the chart. Then close the chart and see what happens.

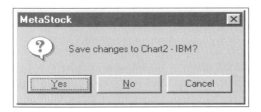

Yep... do we want to save the changes (click the '<u>Y</u>es' button)? If we do, then we can load this chart again with the trendline on it, otherwise it will be lost.

For this exercise, choose '<u>Y</u>es' and save the chart. Name it something meaningful, or something you will remember, I called mine 'IBM 2'!

From here we will follow the steps to open a Smart Chart, the only difference being that when we get to the 'Open' dialog box, we are going to change the 'Files of <u>t</u>ype:' (using the drop down menu) to 'Charts (*.mwc)'. So this is what I see:

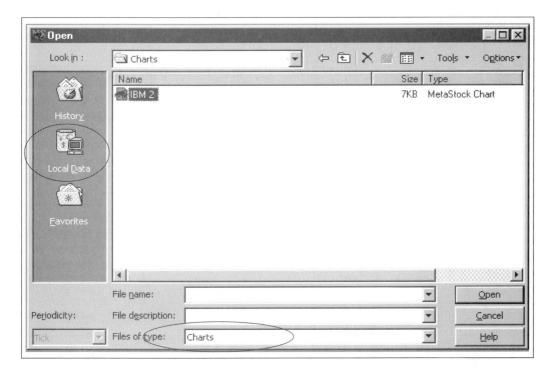

And there is my 'IBM 2' chart, which I can now open. Presto... and there it is complete with trendline. If I make further changes to it, I will be prompted to save those changes when I close the chart.

Now, to summarize the differences between Smart Charts and regular charts:

➤ Smart Charts automatically save any changes made to them.

➤ Regular Charts need to be created and named before they can be saved.

➤ You are prompted to save changes made to a Chart.

There is one last item to cover for Smart Charts. You may be 'experimenting' with a Smart Chart and, somehow, manage to make a complete mess of it. Don't panic! All you need to do is create a new Chart and then save it as a Smart Chart. Let me step you through that as I know it is something I find very useful (and I'm sure you will too!).

Fixing a Smart Chart

Step One: Don't panic (just making sure)!

Step Two: Close the messed-up Smart Chart.

Step Three: Use the 'New Chart' option from either the 'File' drop down menu or the little icon to create a new clean fresh Chart of the messed-up security that the Smart Chart was based on.

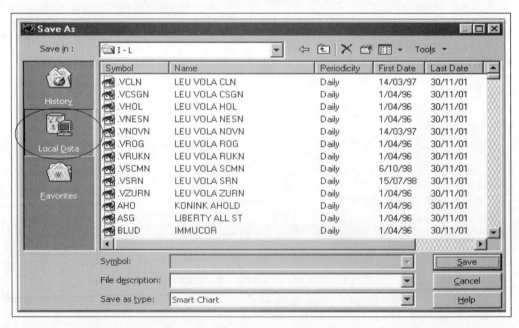

Step Four: Now that you have a new chart open, select 'Save As…' from the 'File' drop down menu.

Step Five: Change the 'Save as type:' to 'Smart Chart' and click the 'Save' button.

Step Six: Click on 'Yes' to replace the existing Smart Chart.

And that's it. You will now have a nice new Smart Chart to work with and if anything happens to it, you know you can always replace it.

Also note that if you somehow end up with a Chart that doesn't look quite how you want it to, as though something has gone wrong with it, just close it down and create a new one—easy!

Different Styles of Charts

By default, MetaStock plots all the charts as bar charts. However, during your charting life, you may want to look at other types of charts. Fortunately, MetaStock allows you to do this. In fact, you can use any of the following styles for your charts:

➤ Bars (High Low Close—which is the common Open, High, Low, Close bar chart).

➤ Candlesticks.

➤ Candlevolume.

➤ Equivolume.

➤ Line.

➤ Kagi.

➤ Point & Figure.

➤ Renko.

➤ Three Line Break.

Certainly the most popular of these would be the Bar, Candlestick, Line and Point & Figure styles, although in recent times Kagi charts have gained in popularity too. (See *Beyond Candlesticks* by Steve Nison.)

We have three ways to change the style of the chart we are using. The first way is to access the 'Prices…' option from the 'Format' drop down menu to bring up the 'Securities Properties' box.

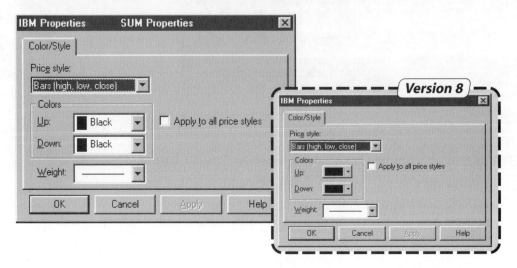

Clicking on the 'Price style:' drop down box will allow you to change the style of the chart.

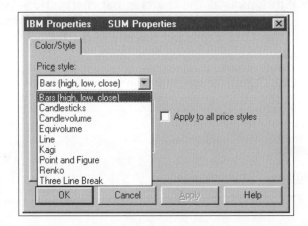

Select the style of chart you require and click the 'OK' button.

Another way to bring up the same 'Properties' box is to double click on the price plot on the chart, or right click on the price plot and select the 'Properties…' option from the short cut menu this brings up (see example opposite).

Either way will bring up the actual 'Properties' box and let you change the style of the chart.

...needs the Style Toolbar. We saw this ...en (see pages 8 and 9). Check your ...nu to make sure it has a check mark ...ere on the screen.

...plot by clicking on it, one click with ... button will do. You will know it is ...se of the little black boxes (handles) ...enly appeared on the price plot. This ...pened earlier too, when you double ...clicked on the price plot.

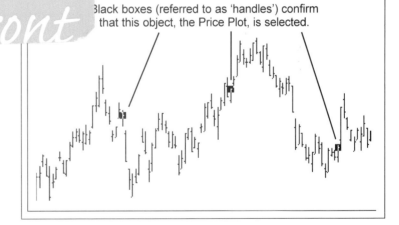

Black boxes (referred to as 'handles') confirm that this object, the Price Plot, is selected.

Click on the Style Toolbar to select the appropriate chart style.

Let's leave the chart as a bar chart for now and see what else we can change.

Setting Up the Screen

By right clicking in the Main Chart Window, you will see the right click menu.

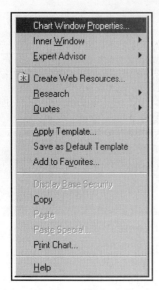

What we want to look at here is the 'Chart Window Properties…'. This lets us set up the screen to appear how we like it, although I think by default, MetaStock does a pretty good job of setting up the screen for us.

However, if there are things we want to change about it, like the title bars or the scale locations, this is where we do it.

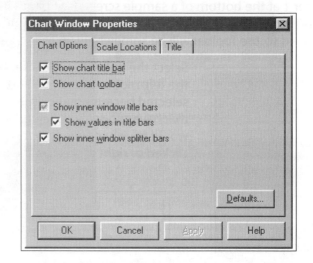

You can select and de-select these options to see what happens. Also, in the 'Scale Locations' tab, you can specify where you want the scale to be displayed, either on the right, left or both. Plus, you can also turn off the 'Date (x-axis)'.

If things go really 'shaky', you can always re-create your chart, so experiment to your heart's content.

Changing the Scales—In Our Favor?

Now, we have two ways of accessing the Properties box for the X and Y scales. The first way is from the 'Format' drop down menu (see opposite). From here you can choose the 'X-Axis…', the 'Right Y-Axis…' or the 'Left Y-Axis…'.

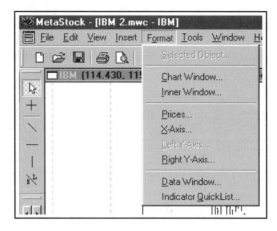

Let's look at the 'X-Axis Properties' box.

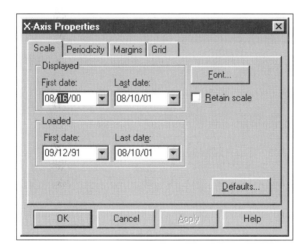

Probably the most useful thing here at this stage is the Grid tab. You can play around with the other options, or just remember that they are here and come back to them at a later stage. Anyway, via the Grid tab, we can turn the grid lines on or off for the X-Axis.

This works the same for the Y-Axis, although the Y-Axis has fewer properties to adjust (see overleaf).

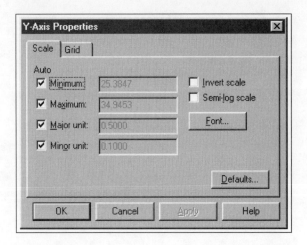

The 'Invert Scale' is a fun thing to try, you can make all the stocks look like they are going up or down—regardless of the price. Note the Y-Axis on the following chart!

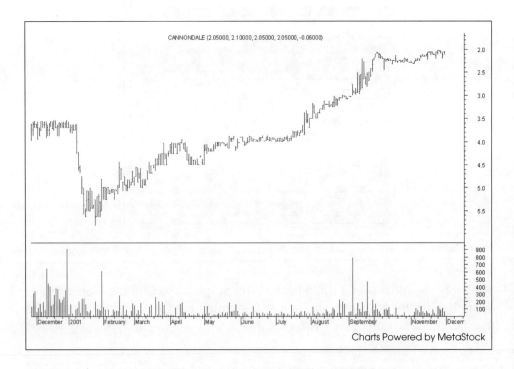

This is also where you can change the scale from linear to semi-log.

So, at least we now know how to get rid of the grid lines, plus how to do a few other things too!

The Chart Toolbar

The Chart Toolbar gives us access to a few very handy little things.

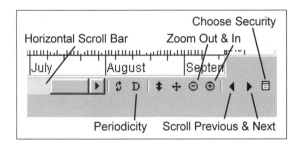

Setting the Chart Period

You can set the Chart's periodicity, i.e. daily, weekly or monthly, etc., by clicking on the Periodicity button—currently showing 'D' for daily.

Zooming

Using the '+' and '–' buttons on the Chart Toolbar allows you to zoom in or zoom out of the chart. You can usually zoom out so far that you have the entire chart on one screen. Alternatively, if you zoom right in, you will have to use the horizontal scroll bar to see the rest of the chart.

Horizontal Scroll Bar

This is at the bottom of the chart, well as long as there is more data loaded than can be displayed on one screen. If not, you won't be able to scroll anywhere.

One really neat little trick with this scroll bar is to hold down the 'Shift' key on the keyboard, whilst clicking on the left or right scroll arrow (on the Horizontal Scroll Bar) to move the chart one period either way.

Let's say you have a daily bar chart on the screen at the moment; well if you haven't, maybe open one up so you can try this. Move the Horizontal Scroll Bar along the bottom of the screen, so you are in about the middle of the chart. Click on the right arrow whilst holding down the 'Shift' key. Notice how the chart moves one day at a time? This is a great way to practice your technical analysis skills to see what you would have done at a certain point, before you actually saw what happened on the chart.

Drawing on the Chart

Trendlines

Well, we know how to draw trendlines and move them, but it might also be useful to know how to delete them. Easy to do if we know the 'right click trick'.

Right clicking on an object brings up a small menu of things we can do with that object (in this case a trendline). We saw this earlier with the 'Chart Window Properties' box.

To remove the trendline, right click on it and select 'Delete' from the sub-menu. The other way to delete the trendline is to select it by left clicking on it (the little squares—'handles'—at the ends of the lines will confirm it is selected) and then hit 'Delete' on the keyboard.

When you delete something from a chart, Metastock makes you confirm what you are doing. You can turn the 'Confirm deletion of objects' off and on via the 'General' tab in the 'Options...' menu in the 'Tools' drop down menu. It's a good idea to leave this feature on as one day you might need it! It's really a double check, just to make sure you really want to delete something.

From the right click sub-menu, we can also select the properties of the trendline. This is useful for changing the color and style of the line.

Here is another useful little trick for all you options traders who like to plot options on a chart. If you have trouble getting the line in exactly the right spot, simply go into the 'Trendline Properties' box and fill it in as follows:

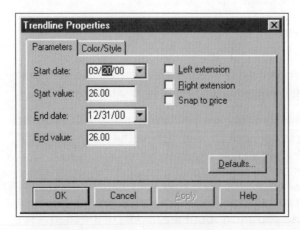

➤ The 'Start date:' is the date you purchased the option.

➤ The 'End date:' is the expiry date.

➤ The 'Start value:' and 'End value:' are the strike price.

This will give you a nice straight line in exactly the right place!

Horizontal Lines for Support and Resistance

On the same toolbar as the trendline, you will also find another very useful line tool—the horizontal line.

This line is typically used for drawing support and resistance lines on your chart, which represent areas where the price struggles to push up or down through. Try this now! Open a chart and then select the Horizontal Line icon and position it on the chart. Once you have put it on the chart, you can select it again and move it up or down. The 'Properties' box (accessed by double clicking on the line) gives you access to the 'Parameters' and 'Color/Style' sections. Here you can color the lines, etc. and also enter the exact value of the line—this can be easier than moving it up and down on the chart, trying to get it on the exact price level! On the chart below, you can see I have used two horizontal lines, one as support and the other as resistance. This is just one of the many uses for the horizontal line tool.

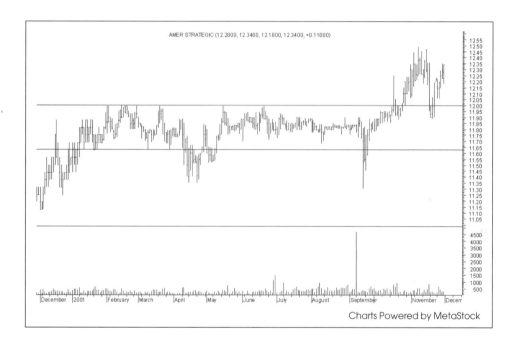

Charts Powered by MetaStock

Text and Symbols

Wow... this is just like having a big piece of paper in front of you, all ready to draw on! You can write on it too. If you have a look at the Text Toolbar, you will see options for text ('abc'), a grid that gives you access to a whole palette of symbols, and a variety of shapes to add to your charts. Let's see what we can do. The chart overleaf shows the result.

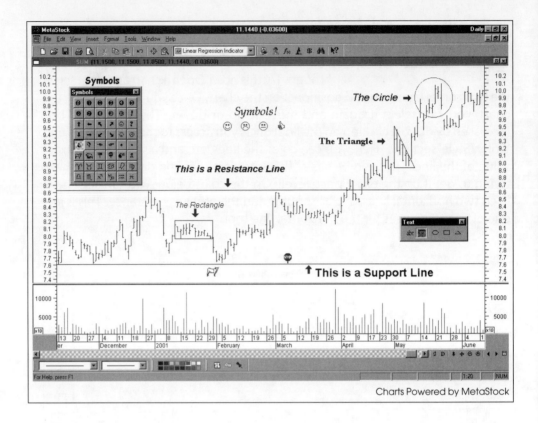

Charts Powered by MetaStock

Well, this chart has everything!! You can see some of the symbols available as well as the geometric shapes and the text. I have changed the properties to show you some of the effects that are available, like using different fonts for the text.

Summing Up

So that's it for our first steps at doing things. Let's see what we covered:

➤ We discovered that some charts are smarter than others.

➤ We know what to do if Smart Charts and Charts get 'messed up'.

➤ We can look at different styles of charts.

➤ The screen can be made to look how we want it to look.

➤ The grid lines can be removed.

➤ We can flip the chart upside down without moving the monitor.

➤ The period of the chart can be changed.

➤ We can scroll through the chart one period at a time.

➤ Charts can be zoomed in and out.

➤ It's easy to draw trendlines and move them… and even delete them.

➤ There is a neat little trick to plot options contracts.

➤ It's easy to draw horizontal lines.

➤ There are various options we can use to annotate our charts with text, symbols and shapes.

3

Indicators,
Where the Fun Really Starts

 **IN A NUTSHELL** we will cover:

Plotting indicators over the price chart.

Plotting indicators in their own personal window.

Changing the indicator properties and how to delete indicators.

Plotting indicators based on volume.

Scaling Options.

Setting up the QuickList with our favorite indicators.

Wiping the slate clean to start again!

MetaStock has over 100 built-in ready-to-run indicators.

This is it, you're up to the chapter on using indicators! It probably feels like you have been working through this book for ages to get to this much-awaited chapter. Well, wait no further—let's get plotting!

One of MetaStock's many strengths is the number of indicators that it has available. Couple this with the ability to create or build your own super powerful indicators and it's no wonder people think MetaStock is just so good. For those people who want to 'BYO'—build your own—the next chapter will step you through how to create a MetaStock approximation of the Alan Hull Range Indicator.

Plotting Indicators

Start by creating a New Chart, opening a saved Chart or opening a Smart Chart for this exercise. In this case, take the easy option and create a New Chart!

Now somewhere on the screen you should see this drop down menu:

Its exact location will depend on how you have your screen set up. This is the Indicator QuickList. From here, we can access all the built in and custom indicators.

Click on the drop down arrow to reveal the lengthy list of available indicators.

Select an indicator by clicking on it and notice that the mouse pointer changes to a hand. This allows you to drag and drop the indicator. For this example, I've chosen the Bollinger Bands. Now, with the left mouse button held down, drag the mouse onto the chart (the pointer changes to a line chart). Release the mouse button and you will see the 'Properties' box for that particular indicator.

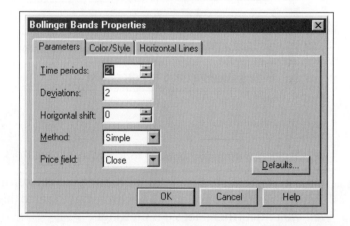

Click the 'OK' button and the indicator will be plotted. It will also now be showing up in the Indicator QuickList, ready to be dragged and dropped again. (Note: If the 'Scaling Options' box pops up, select 'Merge with scale on right'.)

Your screen might then look something like the example opposite, although it will of course depend on what security you have chosen and the indicator you plotted.

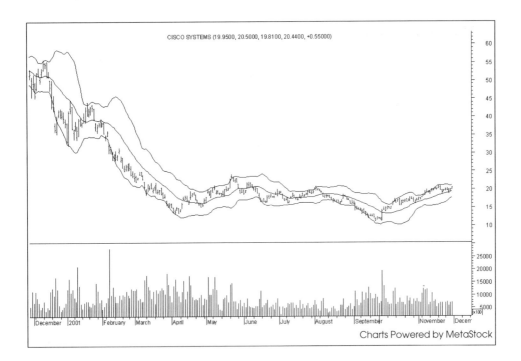

CISCO SYSTEMS (19.9500, 20.5000, 19.8100, 20.4400, +0.55000)

Charts Powered by MetaStock

When you dragged the mouse down over the chart, you probably noticed that the price plot (in this case a bar chart) changed color from black (maybe to bright pink or magenta). This tells you that the indicator will be calculated based on the values of the price plot. We will see shortly that this can be different if we want to plot a moving average on volume as opposed to the stock price.

Before we get into changing the indicator's properties, we can look at another way to plot an indicator. Again, select an indicator from the Indicator QuickList.

This time I've chosen 'Directnl Movement +DI'. Now when you drag it down, notice that when the pointer is over the Main Chart or Inner Window Title Bar (refer back to Chapter 1, pages 8 and 9), the pointer changes to show a window as well as the line. This means that at that point, if we release the button, the indicator will be plotted in its own window… all by itself! This is great for plotting things like the Directional Movement Indicators as it is easier to read them without seeing the price plot. Some indicators however, like Bollinger Bands, need to be plotted over the price plot to enable us to interpret them. Others are best plotted in their own window, it's up to you to decide how you want to plot them and what is easiest for you.

Anyway, let's finish off the Directional Indicators. Plot the +DI in its new window. When you release the mouse, change the color of the line in the 'Properties' box (try black) in the 'Color/Style' tab—there is a drop down box which provides a variety of colors.

The screen should look something like this, although again it will depend on what security you have plotted:

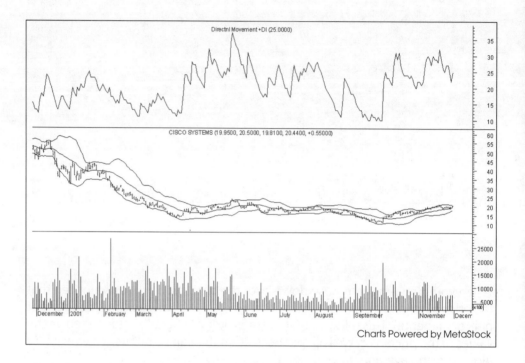

Charts Powered by MetaStock

Now for the -DI, select 'Directnl Movement -DI' from the Indicator QuickList, drag the mouse into the window with the +DI and release—change the color this time to red. (Note: if the 'Scaling Options' box pops up, select 'Merge with Scale on Right'—more on this on page 42.) Do the same for the ADX (select 'Directnl Movement ADX' from the QuickList, drag and drop, etc.) and make it green. You have now plotted the three lines that make up the Directional Movement system and the screen will look very similar to that shown opposite.

Of course the colors don't really show up too well in black and white, but hopefully you have got the general idea. Well done—you are now an Indicator Plotting Expert!

But wait up, we haven't finished yet, there's more to come—like how to change the properties of the indicator and how to delete indicators.

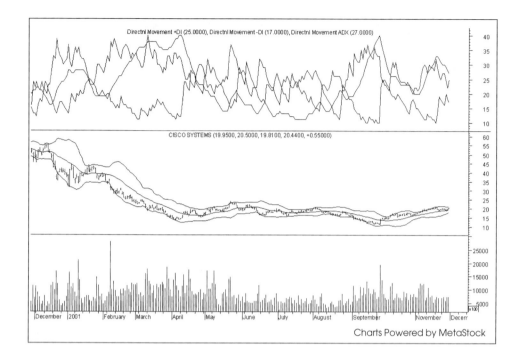

Charts Powered by MetaStock

Changing Indicator Properties and How to Delete Them

Before we go on, close down all the Charts you have open (it's best not to save any changes at this stage) and open up a fresh Chart—a New Chart will do. On this one, we are going to plot a Moving Average indicator and then change the time period of the Moving Average using the 'Properties' box.

Select the Moving Average from the Indicator QuickList and plot it over the price plot (rather than in a separate window)—remember, just drag and drop it over the price plot.

When you let go of the mouse button, the 'Moving Average Properties' box will appear.

In this box, select an appropriate time period for the Moving Average. (I picked 30, but any number greater than 2 will do!) Then select the type of Moving Average —I picked Exponential (see Chapter 11, 'Further Reading and Stuff!' for books on technical analysis if this is all way too confusing for you!).

For now, leave the other parameters as they are, with the exception being the Color in the 'Color/Style' tab, which you can choose to suit your tastes.

Moving Average Properties ☒

| Parameters | Color/Style | Horizontal Lines |

Time periods: 30

Vertical shift %: 0

Horizontal shift: 0

Method: Exponential ▼

Price field: Close ▼   Defaults...

[OK] [Cancel] [Apply] [Help]

This is my chart now:

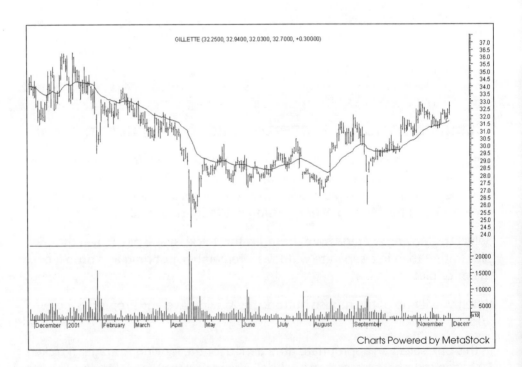

Wouldn't it be great if we could now easily change the time period of the moving average without having to re-plot it? Or even change the type, making it a Simple Moving Average? Or what about changing it so it uses the high price for the day, rather than the closing price? Well, in MetaStock we can... and it's quick and easy too.

To access the 'Moving Average Properties' box once the indicator is plotted, double click on the Moving Average line. The 'Properties' box will open up and the Moving Average line itself will have little black boxes—'handles'—on it, showing that it is selected or active (we saw this earlier with the 'handles' on the price plot). Change the time period to, say, 150 either using the up and down arrows or by typing the number in and click the 'OK' button. Sit back and marvel at your achievements. You now have a 150-day/week/month Moving Average (depending on the chart's periodicity).

From the 'Properties' box, we could also change the color and style of the line and the type of Moving Average. In fact, the parameters in the 'Properties' box will vary depending on the indicator we are plotting. With some indicators, there are more variables to finetune than with others. The MetaStock Help screen will give you full details of the various parameters and what they mean.

OK, now that we have our Moving Average plotted, let's delete it. Select the line, making sure the little black boxes or 'handles' show up. Once selected, it can be deleted by hitting 'Delete' on the keyboard. The other way to get rid of it would be to right click on the Moving Average line (selecting it) and then clicking on 'Delete' in the sub-menu.

We could keep plotting Moving Averages and create, for instance, the Guppy Multiple Moving Average (MMA); however, that is going to keep for Chapter 6 which will deal with making Templates.

What we will do now is plot a Moving Average based on volume instead of price. I won't go into too much detail, just the basic steps:

Step One:	Select the Moving Average from the Indicator QuickList.
Step Two:	Drag and drop the indicator over the volume plot – see how the volume plot changed color.
Step Three:	Select the appropriate Properties – notice that the Price Field now shows 'Indicator'.
Step Four:	Select 'Merge with scale on right' on the Scale Options (if it appears).

You have now plotted a Moving Average based on volume.

Scaling Options

Time now to clarify the Scaling Options.

When you plot some indicators, this box pops up asking what scale you want to use. Depending on how you work, the price will be plotted either using the right-hand scale or the left-hand scale or both. When you plot an indicator, you can then select what scale you want to use, or none at all ('Overlay without scale').

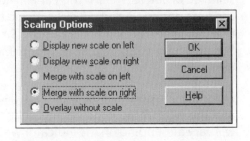

As to what you choose, well like most things it's up to you. However there a few things to keep in mind. Some indicators like Williams %R have values between 0 and -100, therefore it's not much good plotting them on the same scale as the price plot! You can try it... I did, sometimes these things are best learnt by actually doing! Williams %R is best plotted on a new scale or without any scale, or even better yet, in its own separate window. On the other hand, indicators like Moving Averages are best plotted on the same scale as the price plot. If you don't, when you zoom in and out of the chart you will find that the point where the Moving Average line crosses with the price plot will change—this can be very annoying if your trading system is based on when the closing price crosses with a Moving Average!!

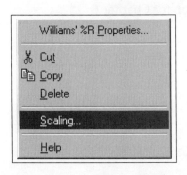

If you have plotted an indicator and would like to change what scale it uses, don't worry, MetaStock lets you do that by right clicking on the indicator to access the right click menu.

Clicking on the 'Scaling...' then brings up the 'Scaling Options' box we have just seen.

Customizing the Indicator QuickList

OK, now that we are all plotted out, what we might do is customize the Indicator QuickList. After all, few people really need to see all those indicators on the drop down list. It sort of makes sense to only have the ones we really need or use showing up. Don't worry if you change your mind about what Indicators show up, you can always change it back to how things were, so nothing is lost.

To customize the Indicator QuickList, select 'Indicator QuickList...' from the 'Format' drop down menu.

You'll see the 'QuickList Properties' box like this:

Now it's fairly easy to pick and choose the indicators you want to show up in the drop down list. Start by clicking on the 'Uncheck All' button and then select those you want. If you change your mind and want all of them, click on 'Check All'. You'll work out over time which indicators you want in your list, or maybe you like to tinker with all of them—with MetaStock, the decision is yours.

Help... the Screen's a Mess!

The last thing to cover in this chapter is a bit of troubleshooting.

You may find from time to time that when you are deleting things from your charts, you get carried away and end up with something that may look a little bit like this:

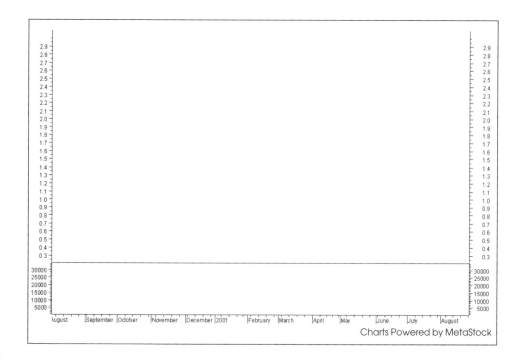

UH-OH!! Where has everything gone and how do we get it back? When the price plot was 'inadvertently' deleted, there would have been a message to say that to plot it again, select 'Display <u>B</u>ase Security' from the right click menu.

OK, so that gets the price plot back… but what about the volume? Well, volume is plotted as an indicator, so you can select it from the Indicator QuickList and plot it on the chart somewhere.

All this is a bit messy because usually you have to re-format windows as well to get things looking the same as they used to. The much, much easier way is to start all over again and create a new chart! This can then be saved as the Smart Chart and everything's back to normal. (You may remember how we did this in the last chapter.) Another way would be to apply the Default Template, but wait until we have covered Templates before trying that one (see Chapter 6).

Finally, a very quick word of warning about plotting indicators. Now that you can do it and know how easy it is to plot them, you may be tempted to get a bit 'carried away' with it all. This can lead to charts that look something like the following—a very sad case of 'too many indicators spoil the chart'!

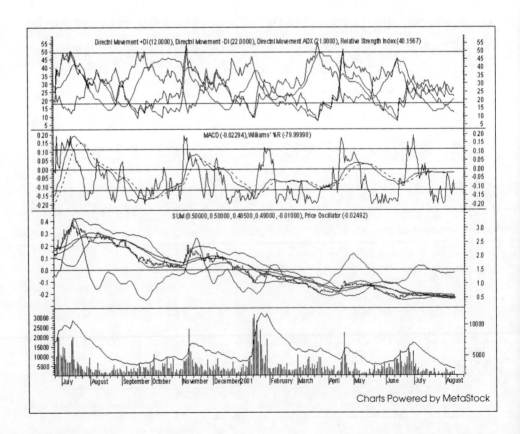

Charts Powered by MetaStock

Again, if this gets too out of hand, simply close the Chart down and start again, or in the case of a Smart Chart—re-create it and replace it.

I guess there is a moral to this story and that is, no matter what mess you make of your chart, you can always wipe the slate clean and start again… what a relief!!

Now it's time to move on and do a bit of indicator building. We'll come back to plotting indicators a bit later when we look at templates and shortcuts to plotting your favorite indicators.

We've covered a lot in this chapter and you are now certainly well equipped to actually do something productive with MetaStock.

4

Build Your
Own Indicator

 **IN A NUTSHELL** we will cover:

Building the MetaStock approximation of Alan Hull's Range Indicator (Central Cord, Upper Deviation and Lower Deviation).

Alan Hull's description of his Range Indicator.

Building another very quick indicator of questionable usefulness — because it is easy to do!

Building an indicator that shows when the closing price is above the 150-day Moving Average.

Now if only I had an indicator that did....

This chapter is going to dump you right into the deep end... it's time to build your own indicator. You may wonder why we would build more, MetaStock already has so many in it. Well, firstly it's fun and secondly, sometimes there are new indicators created that aren't in MetaStock, that's why MetaStock has this facility, a way of future-proofing the software.

MetaStock Formula Language

The MetaStock Formula Language is a MetaStock-specific programming language that is used in the following tools:

➤ Expert Advisor.

➤ Indicator Builder.

➤ System Tester.

➤ Explorer.

It is roughly based on a spreadsheet programming language, like that in Microsoft's Excel. Programming the tools requires using the built-in functions in conjunction with mathematical operators. Help on all the functions can be found in the MetaStock manual or via the Help screens. In Help, you will find details of what the functions actually do as well as what parameters are required. For those with no programming experience in either a programming language or using a spreadsheet, the going may get tough as you are on a fairly steep learning curve. The following examples, however, can easily be typed in and used, even if you are not sure of how to actually create them from scratch.

Alan Hull's Range Indicator

First we are going to build the MetaStock approximation of Alan Hull's Range Indicator (www.alanhull.com).

Alan is well known for his *Charting in a Nutshell* book and his Active Investing strategy which teaches people how to invest in blue chip shares. We'll just go ahead now and build the indicator and then read what Alan has to say about it.

Here's a summary of what we need for this indicator (all will be explained after we've built it):

➤ Central Cord—13-week Linear Regression line based on the closing price.

➤ Upper Deviation—Central Cord plus 3 times the Average True Range.

➤ Lower Deviation—Central Cord less 2.5 times the Average True Range plus a few conditions.

Again, if some of these terms are unfamiliar to you, see the 'Further Reading' section in Chapter 11 for details of helpful technical analysis books.

Let's start up the Indicator Builder. This can be done via the Standard Toolbar or the Tools drop down menu. Here's the Toolbar:

Now we have the main Indicator Builder screen:

Click on 'New…' to create a new Indicator.

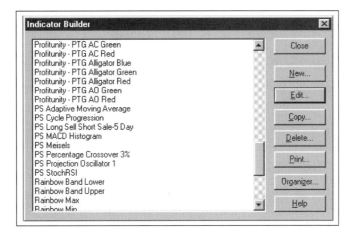

From here we can start entering the code, the MetaStock Formula Language.

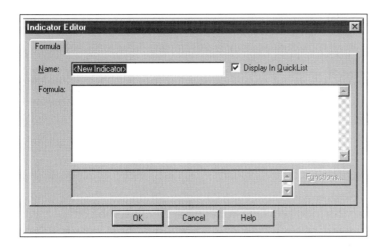

We'll call it 'AH Range C', so type this into the 'Name:' field. Leave the check mark in the 'Display in Quicklist' box, that way the Indicator will show up in the Indicator QuickList.

We won't be going into great detail about the various MetaStock functions, you can either read the manual or check the online help. So for now just type the following into the 'Formula' box:

LinearReg(C,13)

The MetaStock Linear Regression function and its parameters are:

LinearReg(data array, period)

Data array: In this example this is the closing price (represented by 'C').

Period: The timeframe to be used, 13 in this case to represent 13 weeks (make sure the chart periodicity is set to 'W' for weeks).

It should look like this:

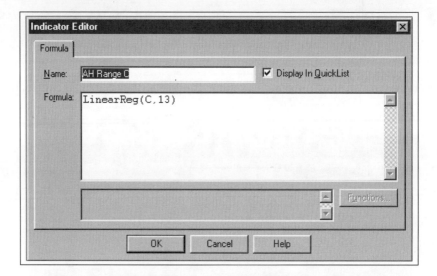

Click 'OK' to close the window, then 'Close' the 'Indicator Builder' dialog box. Now select it from the Indicator QuickList (it will be at the bottom of the list with the other 'Custom Indicators') and plot it! Congratulations… you have now built and plotted an indicator. (Please don't get too excited as this one is already available from the QuickList as a built-in indicator—still it does give one a sense of achievement.)

Let's do it all again and this time call it 'AH Range U'. The code for the upper deviation is:

LinearReg(C,13)+(ATR(13)*3)

This adds 3 times the 13-period Average True Range (ATR) to the 13-week Linear Regression line.

The Average True Range function in MetaStock, and its only parameter, is shown at the top of the next page.

ATR(Period)

Period: The number of time periods to use – we are using 13 for 13 weeks.

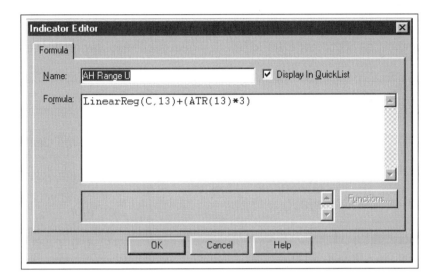

Plot this one and you should have something that looks like this:

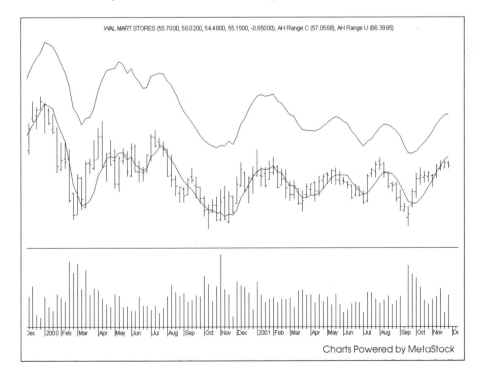

For these examples, make sure the chart periodicity is set to 'W' for weeks as the formulas are based around a weekly chart. You can change the colors of the lines too, as discussed in the previous chapter. Also make sure that the indicators and price are all plotted on the same scale, otherwise the interpretation will be meaningless (remember in this case we will be analyzing where the stock price is in relation to the indicator).

It gets a little trickier now. The Lower Deviation has some 'conditions' attached to it. To make it easier to understand how it works, see the following flow chart:

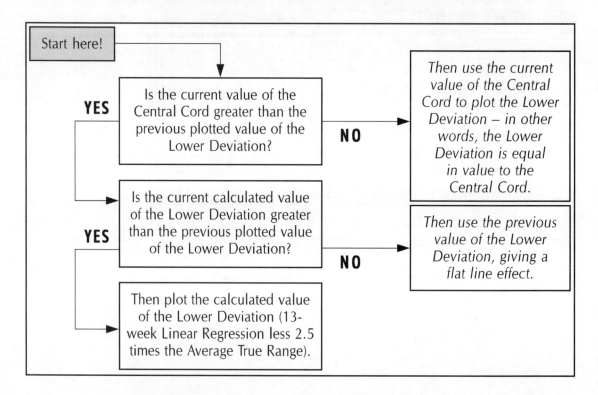

Open the Indicator Builder again and create a new Indicator, let's call it 'AH Range L'. Now, don't try to understand the following code, just trust me that it does exactly what is in the flow chart above. Enter this in the 'Formula:' box as one complete line with no hard returns:

```
If(LinearReg(C,13)>PREV,If(LinearReg(C,13)-(ATR(13)*2.5)>PREV,LinearReg
(C,13)-(ATR(13)*2.5),PREV),LinearReg(C,13))
```

To enable the program to make decisions, we have used the MetaStock 'If' statement.

The format for the 'If' statement is:

If (condition true or false, if true do this, if false do this)

In this example we have 'nested' the 'If()' statements to make decisions within decisions! There is a simpler example of using the 'If()' statement on page 55. But for now, just keep going with this one. This is what you should now have on the screen:

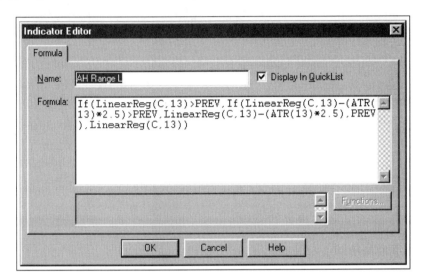

And when you plot this part of the Indicator, combined with the other two, it should look something like this:

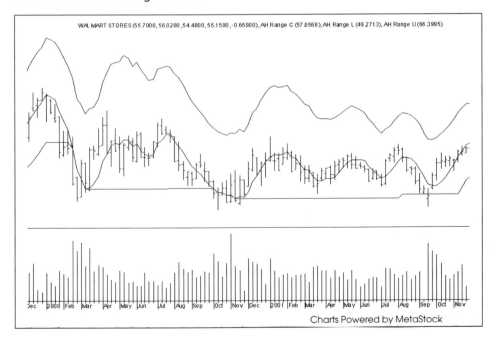

You have now built and plotted the three lines that make up Alan Hull's Range Indicator. Please note as mentioned earlier, this is only an approximation of Alan's indicator, due to limitations with the MetaStock Formula Language.

When plotting the three lines, it is best to plot the Central Cord last, that way when the Central Cord and Lower Deviation are equal, you will only see the Central Cord.

The three lines could all be programmed in as one indicator, however the downside of doing this is that the lines will all be the same color (although recent versions of MetaStock allow you to color individual lines in a multi-plot indicator).

OK, now we've done the 'difficult stuff', we may as well find out a bit more about what we've just built. Here are a few words from Alan to give you some background on his Range Indicator… over to you Alan!

"Take a look at the chart below. The three lines that we have constructed create what I refer to as the 'Range Indicator' which defines four distinct areas or zones. Our actions will depend solely on which zone the price activity is in.

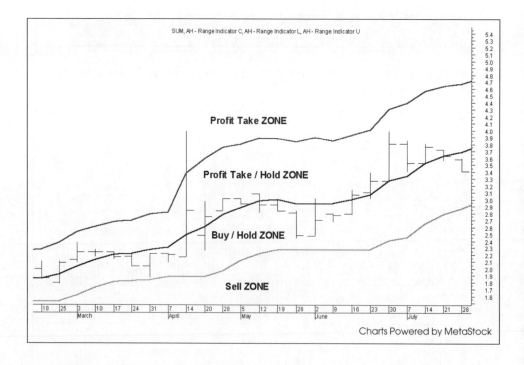

"I refer to the three lines as the Central Cord, the Upper Deviation and the Lower Deviation. The rules I use for the zones are shown opposite.

Sell Zone:	Mandatory – Sell if the share price closes at the end of a week in this zone.
	Optional – Sell if the share closes at the end of a day in this zone.
Buy/Hold Zone:	Buy the share if it has closed at the end of the week in this zone and it has closed up on the previous week's closing price. The purchase price must be between the Lower Deviation and the Central Cord. Hold if already owned.
Profit Take/ Hold Zone:	Hold if the share price is in this zone or profit take by selling if the position is up by 10% per month or more, i.e. 10% in 4 weeks, 30% in 13 weeks, etc.
Profit Take Zone:	Mandatory – Profit take by selling if the share price closes in this zone.
	Optional – Profit take by selling if the share price is in this zone at any time.

"This indicator is universal in terms of timeframe in that it can be applied to daily charts as well as weekly charts and monthly charts. The only adjustment that I make when I switch to daily charts is to vary the period I use between 10 and 20."

Thanks Alan, that's all pretty clear... now we know what each of the lines are.

In Chapter 6, we will create a template based on this indicator so that we can use it again and again, complete with the changed colors. Then in Chapter 8, you will be able to assign the template to a Custom Toolbar button for easy access, all at the click of a button.

Other Ideas

Well, that's just one indicator you can build. Now it's up to your imagination or finding something in a magazine or on the Internet. It's well worth checking out the Equis website (the home of MetaStock) www.equis.com as they have a selection of indicators written by various people and posted to the site. Daryl Guppy's site, www.guppytraders.com, also has several pages of MetaStock formulas (about a dozen or so pages at last count) which can be cut and pasted into MetaStock.

You will probably also get some benefit from examining the Custom Indicators that come with MetaStock. This will give you ideas as to what can be done and how to do it. To do this, start the Indicator Builder, select a particular Indicator and then click on 'Edit'. You can then see the MetaStock Formula Language at work.

If you still haven't got any firm ideas to program in, don't worry, just use the many standard indicators that come with the program—after all, you already have lots to choose from.

OK, well if you really want to try another, here's one that is slightly different. A Custom Indicator for you to plot, in three easy steps:

Step One: Start the Indicator Builder and select 'New' to create a new Indicator.

Step Two: Name the Indicator and type in the following code:

         HHV(H,52);

         LLV(L,52);

Step Three: Click 'OK' and plot the Indicator on a weekly chart.

You have now used the 'Highest High Value' function and the 'Lowest Low Value' function. The Indicator you have just plotted will show you the highest weekly high for the last 52 weeks and the lowest weekly low for the last 52 weeks. The MetaStock functions and the parameters required are:

Highest High Value
HHV(data array, period)

Data array: The field that will be used, which here is the high price or 'H'.

Period: The number of periods used in the calculation—52 in this example, which on a weekly chart means 52 weeks.

Lowest Low Value
LLV(data array, period)

Data array: The field that will be used, which here is the low price or 'L'.

Period: The number of periods used in the calculation—52 in this example, which on a weekly chart means 52 weeks.

But wait, there's one more!

This is a simplified example using the 'If()' statement.

We are going to build an Indicator that plots the value 1 if the closing price is greater than the 150-day Simple Moving Average of the closing price. If it's not, then a 0 will be plotted, i.e. if the closing price is less than or equal to the 150-day Moving Average.

Let's build it and see what it does.

Step One:	Start the Indicator Builder and select 'Ne̲w' to create a new Indicator.
Step Two:	Name the Indicator and type in the following code:
	If(C>mov(C,150,s),1,0)
Step Three:	Plot the Indicator on a daily chart—in its own window.

The new function we have used is the Moving Average, which has parameters as follows:

Mov(data array, period, method)

Data array:	The field that we are using to calculate the moving average, in this example the closing price or 'C'.
Period:	The number of time periods used to calculate the average; here we will use 150.
Method:	This identifies the method to be used, i.e. Simple, Exponential or Weighted; this example is based on a 'Simple' Moving Average, or 'S'.

In this example, you can quite clearly see how the 'If()' statement works.

If C>mov(C,150,s) is true, then plot 1

If C>mov(C,150,s) is not true, then plot 0

When plotted, it should look something like this:

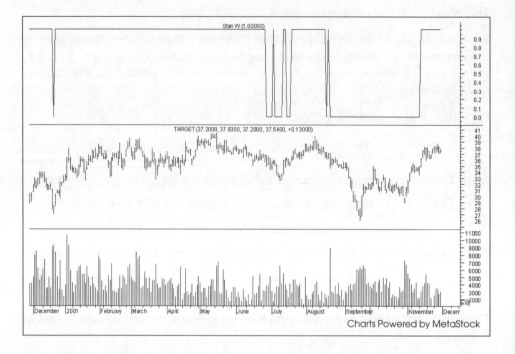

You can also plot the 150-day Simple Moving Average of the closing price on the chart to double check the results.

OK, that's all done. Next we will step through the how and why of setting up a layout, before we move onto templates and looking at an example of how we would build the Guppy Multiple Moving Average (MMA) indicator.

5

Layouts –
Making Multi-Chart Displays

 **IN A NUTSHELL** we will cover:

The use of layouts.

Using the Window drop down menu.

Cloning charts.

How to create a layout.

Adding and deleting charts from a layout.

One chart is fine, but it would be great to see the daily and weekly charts together, or even a group of indexes.

Well, after the work-out of the last chapter, it's probably time to change the pace a bit, just for variety.

As we're becoming more familiar with MetaStock and are thoroughly enjoying the way it has made our charting life so much easier, there are, of course, still things we would like to do. Let's say we want to look at not just one chart, but several charts… all at the same time. In fact we want to look at a daily chart, a weekly chart and a monthly chart… all at once. Hmmmm… how would we do it? Opening up all the charts and selecting 'Tile' from the 'Window' drop down menu would do the trick. Yes… BUT, what if we want to look at that array of charts again, tomorrow, the day after and next week, is there some way MetaStock can help? Of course there is, that's what layouts are for. (I'm sure the MetaStock developers have thought of nearly everything!)

What Layouts Do

Layouts let you create screen displays that include more than one chart, in fact they can have as many as you want. The charts can be of the same security or different securities, the periodicity can be different as can the appearance of each chart. Also, you can arrange the charts to suit and save them in that formation, i.e. tiled or cascaded. As always, the best way to understand all this is to do something practical, so let's make a layout, but before we do, a quick word about the Windows options.

Window Displays

I keep referring to things that MetaStock does as being 'like a normal Windows program'. This is no exception. In fact, even the program I am using to write this book has a 'Window' drop down menu. If you have used this drop down menu in other programs, chances are you will already understand what it does in MetaStock.

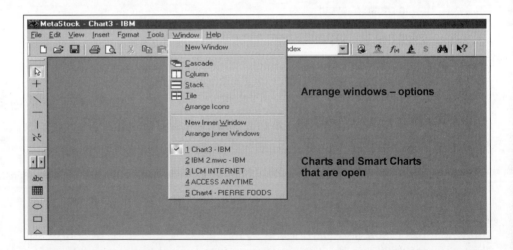

We will be using the 'Tile' option to arrange the charts so they are all visible (just like in other Windows programs).

The 'New Window' option is quite useful as it allows us to 'clone' an existing Chart or Smart Chart, so we end up with another chart that is an identical copy. We will see this in action in the example, so now let's create our first layout.

Creating a Layout

For this example, I want a screen display that has:

➤ A daily bar chart.

➤ A weekly candlestick chart with no volume.

➤ A monthly line chart also with no volume.

I only want a scale on the right side of the charts and I don't want any grid lines!

Right, firstly pick a stock, any stock, and open up a new chart (using 'File', 'New', 'Chart…'). Do it again… and again, or you could clone the chart using the 'New Window' option from the 'Window' drop down menu (that was just discussed).

You now have three charts of stock XYZ. From the 'Window' drop down menu, select 'Tile'. Your screen will look like this:

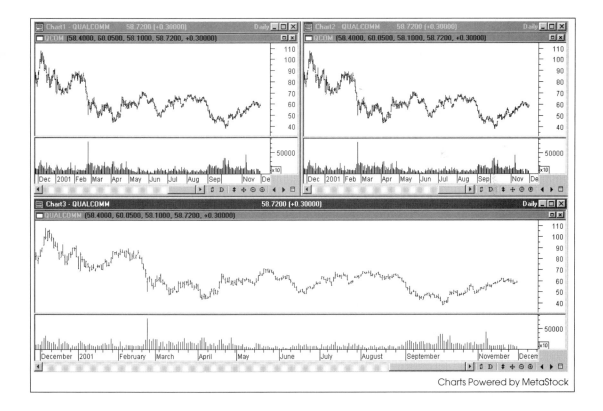

To change the chart styles and periodicity to match what we require, use any of the methods described earlier—try double clicking on the price plot to bring up the 'Properties' box to change each chart's style.

The periodicity is changed via the Chart Toolbar. Click the 'D' for day and then select 'W' (weekly) or 'M' (monthly), as required, from the pop up menu.

Now to delete the Volume, right click in the Volume window to bring up the right click menu. Select 'Inner Window' from the menu and then the 'Close Inner Window' option—the Volume window will be deleted.

Next, we want to make sure we only have the scale on the right-hand side of each chart. To do this, we use the right click menu (as shown in Chapter 2). Right click in the main chart area of each chart and deselect the left scale from the 'Chart Options' tab in 'Chart Window Properties...'.

Finally the grid lines; right click on the X-Axis (or double click on it) to bring up the 'X-Axis Properties' box. From the Grid tab, remove the 'check' from the 'Show Grid' box—this will get rid of the grid lines.

Mission complete! You should now be looking at three charts as follows:

➤ Daily bar chart.

➤ Weekly candlestick chart with no volume.

➤ Monthly line chart with no volume.

➤ No grid lines and a scale only on the right-hand side.

Well done.

Hmmm… there must be more to it? Yes there is, but you've done the hard stuff already. From here, we need to actually create the Layout file. We have the contents, now we have to save them. Select 'Layout' from the 'New' option either from the 'File' drop down menu or from clicking on the 'New' icon. This brings up the 'Layout' box and shows all the charts that are open and what charts are in the layout.

Either '---Add--->' the charts one by one, or click the '---Add All--->' to add them all—makes sense, doesn't it!?

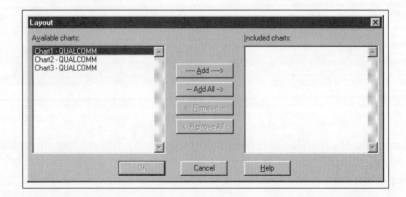

The layout now consists of three charts and looks, or should look, something like this:

Charts Powered by MetaStock

To save it, select either 'Save' or 'Save As…' from the 'File' drop down menu, name it and make sure that 'Save as type:' is 'Layout (*.mwl)' and then you are done… one layout saved to be recalled when required.

Test this out by closing all charts (use the 'Close All' option from the 'File' drop down menu) and then selecting 'Open…' (use either way… whichever you prefer, using the drop down menus is as good as any!) to bring up the 'Open' dialog box. Change the 'Files of type:' box to 'Layouts (*.mwl)' and hopefully you will see the name of the layout you just created. If so, select it and click 'Open'—and there it is. The great thing now is that next week or at whatever time in the future, you can open that layout and see the charts exactly as they appear now—with, of course, updated data in them.

And you don't have to stop there either. You can have more charts in a layout, they can be behind each other, i.e. cascaded, and they can have indicators on them too. Here's another one I prepared earlier (see the screen shot overleaf).

It will be familiar to those of you who have seen Alan Hull's ActVest course and shows the Dow Jones Index, the S&P 500, the Nasdaq and the Australian All Ordinaries (All Ords), with a 9-day and 21-day Simple Moving Average.

Now each day I can call up the layout and see what's happening with the US market and the Australian market—well, at least what's happening with the Moving Averages anyway!

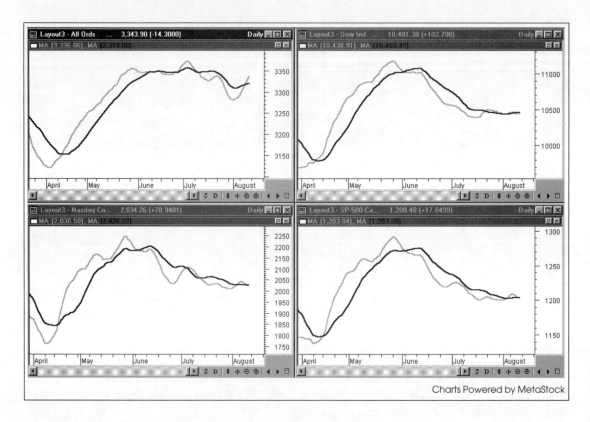

Charts Powered by MetaStock

To create this layout, follow these steps:

Step One: Use 'File', 'New', 'Chart' and create a chart for the:

Dow Jones

S&P 500

Nasdaq

All Ords.

Of course, this assumes that you have the data for these indexes.

Step Two:	Tile the screen.
Step Three:	Plot the Moving Averages on each chart (drag and drop the Indicator and then change the properties, i.e. color, type and time periods).
Step Four:	Delete the base security from each chart.

When you delete the base security, MetaStock will clearly let you know what you are doing. It will also tell you how to get the base security back, which can be very helpful. It's always a good idea to read what is in those little boxes that flash up on the screen, BEFORE you click 'OK'.

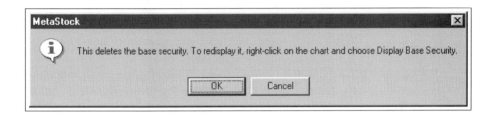

In this case, go ahead and click 'OK'... Okay?

Step Five:	Delete the inner volume window.
Step Six:	Select 'Layout' from 'File', 'New' and '---Add All--->'.
Step Seven:	Go to 'File', 'Save As…' a 'Layout' and name it something appropriate.

Later on, we will connect this Layout to a Custom Toolbar button, so it opens with the click of a button (see Chapter 8).

Editing Layouts

Once you have created a layout, you can add charts to or delete charts from it using 'Edit Layout' from the 'File' drop down menu.

To add a chart (make sure the layout is already open), open the chart, make the changes to it—if any—then go to 'Edit Layout'. You will now see the chart on the left-hand side of the 'Layout' dialog box, ready and waiting to be added into the layout. At this point, you could also remove a chart or charts. Don't forget, though, that if you make any changes to the layout, you will have to save the layout, otherwise all the changes will be lost!

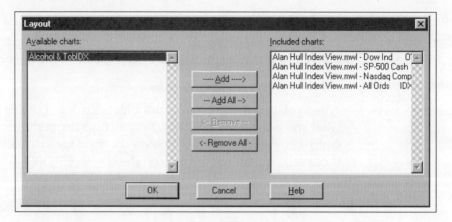

You can also remove charts from a layout by closing the particular chart (click on the 'x' to close it). The option is then to close the entire layout, or just delete that chart from the layout.

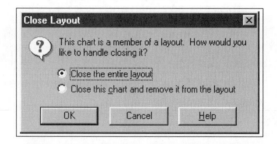

Layouts can be really useful and can save you time. A bit of forward planning and you only have to set some of these things up once and they are done forever (or until your PC crashes!). Please keep in mind that what we have done here and through the book so far are just examples of what you can do. Once you know the power of the MetaStock tools, you can customize the program to suit your own style and requirements.

6

Templates – Making Things Easier

 **IN A NUTSHELL** we will cover:

What a Template is.

How useful Templates can be.

Opening templates using two different methods.

Creating a simple template with a few indicators.

Building an easy-to-use version of the Guppy MMA Indicator.

Creating a multi-chart template based on a layout.

Building a template for Alan Hull's Range Indicator.

Template (n): A wood or metal pattern used to cut out shapes accurately.

Hmmm… not really applicable to MetaStock, is it?! So what are templates in MetaStock and how in the world are they going to make things easier?

What is a MetaStock Template?

A MetaStock template contains information about how to display and what to display on a chart. For example, let's say you have a particular screen setup that you like to use, it may include some indicators, a particular periodicity, or even no price plot! Templates make it easy to re-use particular screen setups over and over. We'll see this at work… then it will be clearer.

Applying a Template

MetaStock comes with many built-in examples of things like indicators and templates, so in actual fact we don't have to create our own, we can just use what is already available. Of course, that wouldn't be half as much fun now would it?! Plus, there are some things we might like to do which are not like any of the built-in extras.

Before we move on and build our very first original template, let's see how we apply templates and test out a few of the built-in ones.

There are two ways to apply a template:

1. By opening a chart with a particular template.

2. By applying a template to a chart after you have opened it.

Opening a Chart with a Template

Bring up the New Chart window (use either the icon or 'File', 'New', 'Chart…' from the drop down menu). In the 'Options' drop down menu (where we looked at the 'Load Options…'—see page 12), you will see the 'Open with Template…' option.

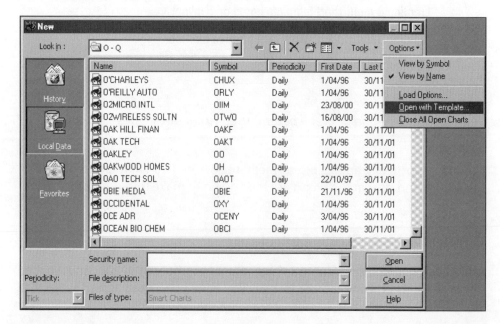

Selecting this option will allow us to choose the template that we want to create our Chart with. Normally, when we create a Chart, MetaStock uses the 'Default' template (which we can apply to a 'severely mutilated' chart to restore it to its original beauty!). We can alter the Default template to create charts the way we want them—I would suggest at this stage it is best to leave the Default template as it is, just in case.

Now pick a template, any one will do for this example. The list of available templates that you see on your screen may differ to what is shown here—it will depend on what version of MetaStock you have, plus the fact that I have already created more templates in my version. Then click 'Open'.

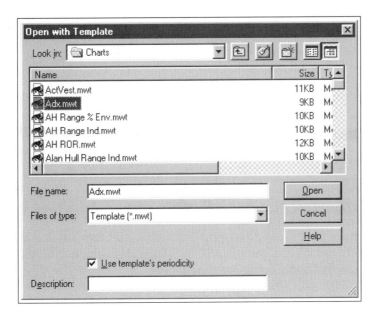

You are then taken back to the 'New Chart' selection screen. Pick your security and click 'Open' in the normal manner and then... hey presto! You have a new chart, created using the template that you selected.

Applying a Template to a Chart that is Already Open

Right click on the chart to bring up the right click menu.

Select 'Apply Template...' to bring up the Apply Template dialog box (examples of both are shown on the next page).

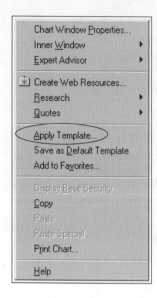

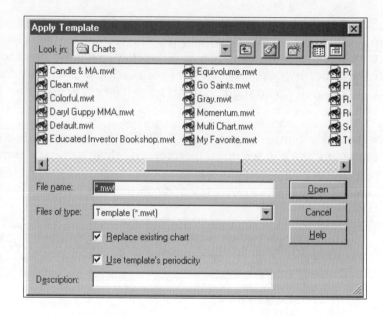

From here we select a template—again, any one will do—then click 'Open'. (If prompted, say 'No' to saving changes to the chart.) WOW! Our plain ordinary chart has been transformed into a brand new chart, based on the template we selected.

Other Options—The Check Boxes

Before we move onto creating a template, multi-chart templates and the Guppy MMA Indicator (which I promised earlier), let me explain the two little check boxes that appear in the 'Apply Template' dialog box:

➤ 'Replace Existing Chart'—This means that when you apply the template, your original chart will be closed. If you don't select this option, then your original chart will still be there as well as the new one based on your template. Try it and see the difference—look at the 'Window' drop down menu to see what charts are available. When this option is not selected, you will see the original chart plus the new one with the template applied.

➤ 'Use Template's Periodicity'—Can be a very useful option. If your template was created as a weekly chart (as my chart was), then when you apply the template, this gives you the option to use the template's periodicity (weekly in my case) or not! Leave it unselected, i.e. no check mark, and your new chart will have the same periodicity as the chart you applied the template to. Again, try this out to see what happens. Remember, if things get totally out of control, you can always create another chart and start again!

Also note that when you use the first method of creating the chart with a template (using 'Open with Template...'), there is no 'Replace Existing Chart' option, which makes sense as we are actually in the process of opening the chart!

Now try either or both methods with a few of the supplied templates to see what they do.

OK, now it's time to create our very own template.

Our First Template

I have set up a screen below to display a weekly candlestick chart, Bollinger Bands plotted over the price plot and the RSI Indicator plotted in a separate window. The scale is on the right side and there are no grid lines.

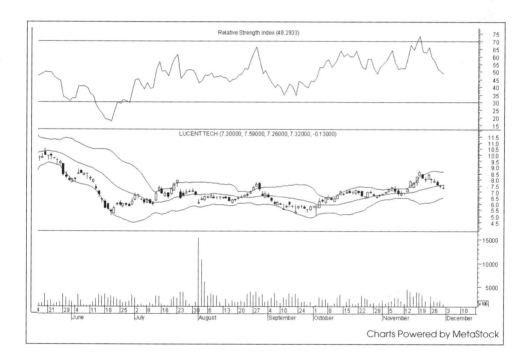

This may be a fairly common screen setup for me, so to enable me to use this repeatedly with ease, I can create a template from this screen. Once created, all I have to do is open a new chart and apply the template and it will display the new chart as a weekly candlestick chart with the RSI and Bollinger bands... just the way I wanted it!

Please bear in mind that this is only an example, you may want to use different indicators or even a different style of chart. You may even want multiple charts (which we will get to soon) or just a screen full of indicators—the choice is yours!

To make a template out of this screen we start by selecting 'Save <u>A</u>s…' from the '<u>F</u>ile' drop down menu which brings up the following 'Save As' dialog box.

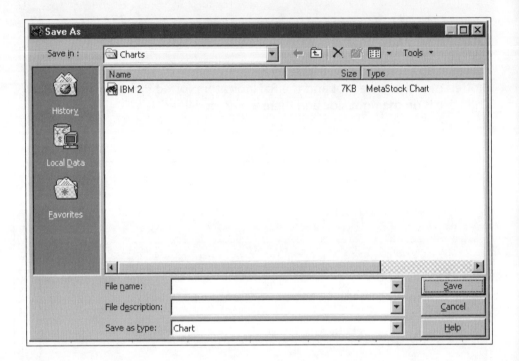

Change the 'Save as <u>t</u>ype:' to 'Template (*.mwt)' via the little drop down box and then key in a name for our template (something appropriate, in my case 'Candle BB RSI'), add a description (optional), click on the '<u>S</u>ave' button and the job's done! You have now created a template that can be applied to any chart.

So now it's time to test it out.

Use one of the methods to apply a template, I would suggest opening a chart and then using the right click menu to apply the template at this stage.

Once applied, the chart will be set up just the way we like it! In my case the chart is now a weekly candlestick chart with the RSI and Bollinger Bands plotted. Templates really are a time-saving device—just another way of automating what you can do in MetaStock.

The Guppy MMA Indicator

You may be familiar with Daryl Guppy, a professional trader, author and teacher. (See www.guppytraders.com for details about Daryl's educational technical analysis newsletter.) You may also be familiar with the Guppy Multiple Moving Average (MMA) that Daryl has developed.

This indicator is made up of two groups of Exponential Moving Averages that represent the behavior of the short-term traders and long-term investors. It delivers powerful messages about the movement of the crowd and its strength—more information about this popular indicator is available in the best-selling book *Trading Tactics* by Daryl Guppy (see Chapter 11 for further reading).

What we are going to do now is plot the Guppy MMA Indicator and then save it as a template for later use. The advantage of using a template for this indicator is that we can change the color of the long-term and short-term groups for easier viewing. We could create an indicator with the two groups of six moving averages, but they would all plot as the same color and it would mean changing the properties each time we plot them—the template is the ideal solution.

Open a new chart and plot the following Exponential Moving Averages of the closing price, based on a daily chart (changing the color to blue or green or any other color you like): 3, 5, 7, 10, 12, 15.

You should see a nice colored band of six Exponential Moving Averages—compare your chart to the chart that I created.

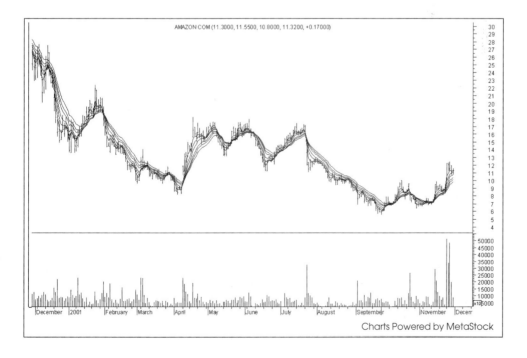

Charts Powered by MetaStock

Now we will add in the long-term group. Plot the following Exponential Moving Averages of the closing price (and use a different color, maybe red): 30, 35, 40, 45, 50, 60.

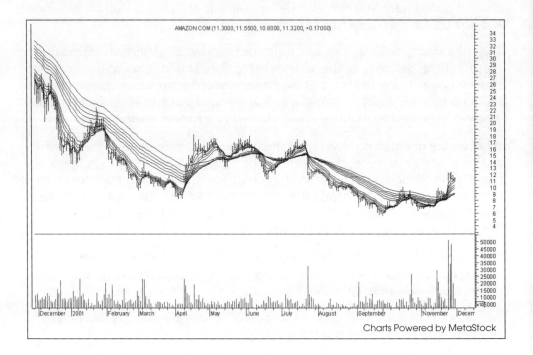

Before we create the template from this chart, we will make a few extra changes to make it more interesting and easier to interpret.

Select the price plot by clicking on it (the little boxes—'handles'—will show up to confirm this). Once selected, use either the right click menu and 'Delete', or hit 'Delete' on the keyboard! Yep… go ahead and delete the base security, just like we did in the last chapter.

Next, right click in the volume window and close it (select 'Inner Window', then 'Close Inner Window'). The screen should now have two bands of exponential moving averages, no price plot and no volume (see the example opposite).

Wouldn't it be great to be able to apply this to any chart? Wouldn't technical analysis be just so much easier if we could click a few buttons and see the Guppy MMA Indicator on any chart?

Well, that's exactly what the template will enable us to do, so let's do it!

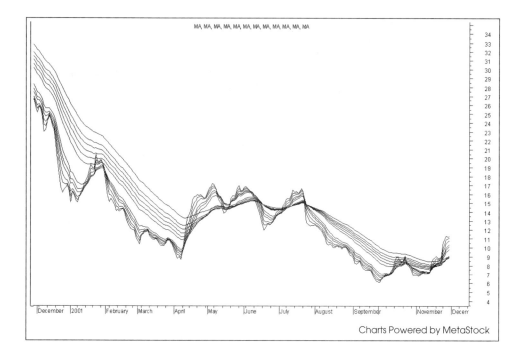

MA, MA, MA, MA, MA, MA, MA, MA, MA, MA, MA, MA

Charts Powered by MetaStock

Select 'Save <u>A</u>s…' from the '<u>F</u>ile' drop down menu and follow the steps outlined previously to save the template (make sure you save it as a 'Template').

If you have version 7.2 of MetaStock or above, you will notice that there is already a 'Daryl Guppy MMA' template in the list of available templates. (You can apply this one and see if what you have created is the same… it should be!)

Open a new chart, apply the template and see the result. Now you can study your Guppy MMA Indicator with ease, any time you want to… MetaStock really does make some of these tasks just so easy.

Multi-Chart Templates

OK, you may be one of these people who like to see more than one chart on the screen at any one time. Well, you would have enjoyed the last chapter on layouts and you now probably have so many charts on the screen you don't know what to do with them! The good news is that we can use a layout as a basis for a template too.

For this example, we will create a layout that shows a daily bar chart, a weekly candlestick chart and a monthly line chart.

The screen looks like this, just like the one we made earlier.

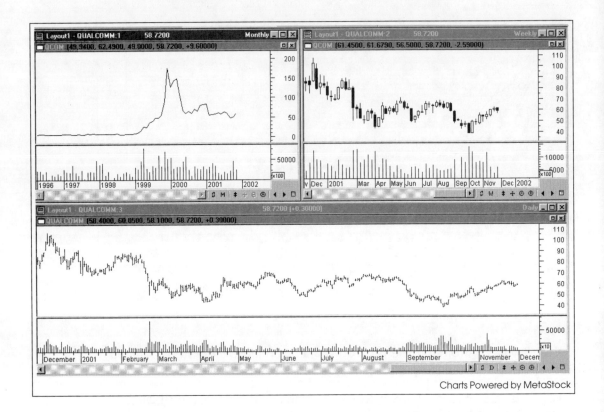

Charts Powered by MetaStock

Follow the same process as for the last template—select 'Save As...' from the 'File' drop down menu, make sure the 'Save as type:' is set to 'Template (*.mwt)', name it and save it (you can add a description here to remind you in the future what the template actually does—quite handy really).

Now open a new chart and apply the template. Your original chart is converted into a multi-chart extravaganza, just the way you wanted it—easy or what?!

Alan Hull Range Indicator Template

You probably have a handle on this now, but just to be sure we'll step through what has to be done for this type of template.

Firstly, create a New Chart or open an existing Smart Chart or Chart. Plot the three indicators we built that make up the Alan Hull Range Indicator. When plotting them, as mentioned previously, plot the Central Cord last.

Change the colors of the lines to something appropriate, maybe green for the Central Cord, blue for the upper deviation and red for the lower deviation. Make any other changes that you like, e.g. delete volume. Don't forget to set the chart periodicity to 'W' for weekly.

When you are happy with the appearance of the chart, save it as a template and name it 'Alan Hull Range Ind' or something similar. You can add a description too, but this is optional.

And that's it!

You can now easily apply the template to any chart.

7

Favorites

 IN A NUTSHELL we will cover:

Why Favorites will be your favorite feature.

How to save Smart Charts to Favorites – including the shortcut.

Scrolling through Favorites.

Using the current chart as a template for the other charts in the folder.

It's OK to Play Favorites With Your Charts

This has to be one of the great 'new' features of MetaStock in recent times. In keeping with the trend of software developers to create standards, MetaStock now includes a 'Favorites' option.

What Favorites Are

Favorites in MetaStock allows you to have your very own personal filing cabinet of all your favorite charts. This is great for setting up watch lists or even keeping track of your portfolio. One of the other great things you will find out about Favorites is that you can scroll through them one by one with the click of the mouse or by using the keyboard shortcut. Think of Favorites as one big filing cabinet for all your favorite charts. You can create as many folders as you like, you can even have folders within folders. We'll go ahead now and create a portfolio

folder in our Favorites, an appropriate place to store, for example, stocks we own—
please note that those shown in the book are just samples.

How to Create Them

Let's open up a Smart Chart (whilst you can save Charts into Favorites, it doesn't
allow you to scroll through them, they need to be of the super smart variety!).
Now to add it to Favorites, right click on the chart to bring up the following menu:

Select the 'Add to Favorites…' option, which brings up the following:

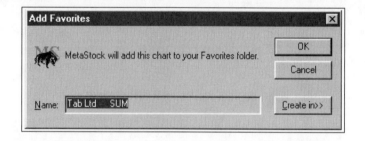

We have two options here:

1. Click the 'OK' button and save the chart to the main
    Favorites directory; or

2. Click on 'Create in>>' **(this does not appear in Version 8)**
    (to allow us to save it in a folder within a folder) which takes
    us to the screen shown below.

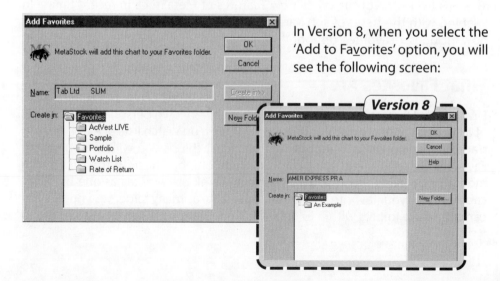

In Version 8, when you select the
'Add to Favorites' option, you will
see the following screen:

OK, so I've already got a few folders in my Favorites directory, you'll probably have none! They are very simple to create, so let's create a sub-folder now.

Click the 'New Folder...' button and enter a name for the folder. Call it anything you like, for this example maybe call it 'An Example', then click 'OK'. You have now created a sub-folder under the Favorites folder. The highlight around the name and the open folder icon mean that this is the selected destination folder for the chart. If you click 'OK' now, the chart will be stored in that folder, in this case the 'An Example' folder. (Version 8 is the same as previous versions except the 'Create in>>' button has been deleted.)

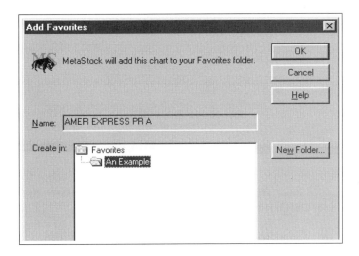

It's a bit like using Windows Explorer to manage your files. As stated previously, any folder you create can have further sub-folders, just don't forget where you've put your favorite chart!

To open the Favorites folder, click on the 'Open' icon, or select 'Open' from the 'File' drop down menu. You will see the usual 'Open' dialog box. Now click on the BIG 'Favorites' button (on the left-hand side—see the image overleaf).

This will show all of the folders within Favorites, plus any charts in the actual Favorites directory. You don't have to use more folders to store your charts in, but it does make them easier to find if you do! Just remember the example of a filing cabinet, no point putting all the documents in one folder, when you can separate them out and be much more organized.

From the 'Open' dialog box, double click on the new folder that's been created and you will see the chart you just saved there. You can open the chart now or just cancel out and come back to it later.

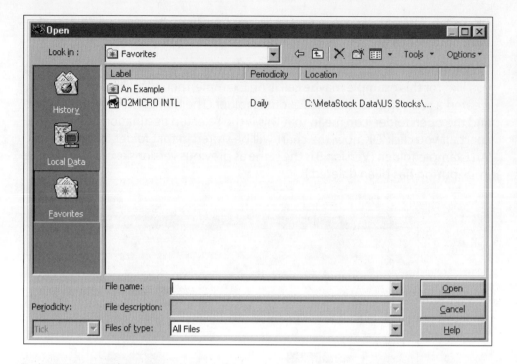

Scrolling Through Favorites

Now moving on, if we have more than one chart in a Favorites folder, we can scroll through them using the forward and back arrows at the bottom of the screen in the Chart Toolbar:

To try this out what we will do is open three or four Smart Charts, add them to our Favorites folder and then open just one and scroll through the rest.

For this I have used a shortcut. Instead of opening the chart and then right clicking on it to add it to the Favorites, I have selected the Smart Charts from 'Local Data' in the 'Open' box and then, using the 'Tools' drop down menu, selected 'Add to Favorites…' (see the example opposite).

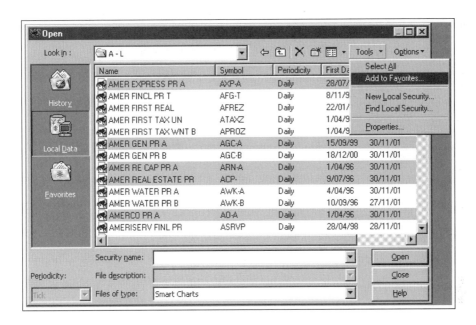

To select multiple charts, use the 'standard' Windows feature for selecting multiple files. As you are clicking on the files, hold down the 'Ctrl' key on the keyboard (the 'Shift' key works too, to select a block of files). This is a quick and easy way to select multiple charts and is the same as selecting multiple files in something like Windows Explorer.

From here, the process to add the charts to your Favorites folder is the same as earlier. Go ahead and add the charts into the folder you made earlier.

Now click on the large 'Favorites' button and go to the folder to which you just added the charts.

The screen shot overleaf shows what my folder looks like now.

OK, this is where it gets exciting…we'll just open one chart and then use the little scroll arrows to see the rest!

Select one of the charts and open it, any chart will do. Now, click on the left or right arrow (that we saw earlier on the Chart Toolbar) and you can scroll through all the charts in that Favorites folder. How useful is that? Well, don't answer yet because there's more! Before we move on, I just want to let you know that there is a keyboard shortcut for the left and right scroll buttons and it is 'Alt' plus the left and right cursor keys. This will work exactly the same as clicking on the scroll arrows on the Chart Toolbar.

Once you've had enough fun scrolling back and forth, come back to the book and we'll do something else.

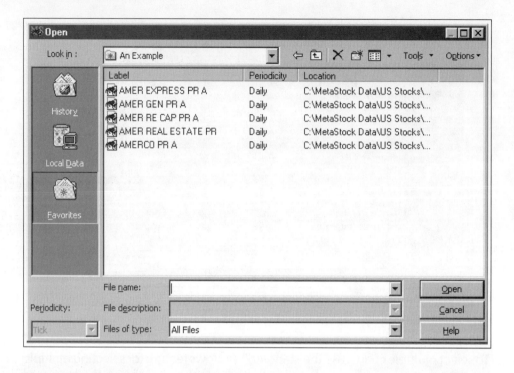

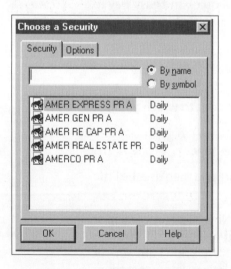

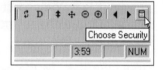

See the little button right down the bottom of the screen on the far right (still on the Chart Toolbar)? It is the 'Choose Security' button.

If you click on this, it will show all the securities available in that particular folder. Click it now and you will see a list of the charts in your current Favorites folder. An example of this is displayed here.

Now we can jump to any chart in the list, instead of scrolling through them all. Again, this is another very useful feature to remember. It's also a quick way of seeing what else is in the current folder—especially if there are a lot of them in the list.

Changing the Appearance of Our Favorites

The last thing we'll cover with Favorites is how to use one of the options in the 'Options' tab of the 'Choose a Security' box.

We have the choice of either scrolling through the charts using the Smart Chart, or we can use the current chart as a template for the other charts in the folder. What does all this mean? Well, let's say you like to look at your portfolio using the Smart Charts, which may have a few indicators on them, etc. Once you have done this, maybe you'd like to see them all with the Guppy MMA or the Alan Hull Range Indicator. To do this, you'd either have to apply a template to each chart as you scroll through, or use one of the options in the err… 'Options' tab!

We'll do this now to make it all nice and clear.

Select the 'Use chart as template' option (you can only select one or the other!) and click 'OK'. Now apply a template to the current chart (which is from your Favorites folder), try the Guppy MMA template that we created earlier—or use the built-in one, or indeed any template. Don't worry about replacing the chart for this exercise and remember you can always revert back to the Smart Chart. Hopefully, you will now see the Guppy MMA chart or whatever other template you used, instead of the original Smart Chart that you had opened.

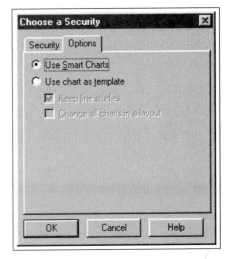

Now when you scroll using the right or left arrow, you will see the Guppy MMA charts instead of the Smart Charts for all the charts in this particular Favorites folder. This is a very convenient way to view a group of charts with different templates. The sky is the limit here! You can create whatever templates you want and then, using this option, scroll through your portfolio or watch list and see the charts with the different templates applied, all the time leaving each Smart Chart intact.

For the more adventurous, you can create a multi-chart template (from a layout) and use it to scroll through your Favorites—just select the 'Change all charts in a Layout' option.

To revert back to being able to scroll through the Smart Charts, select the 'Use Smart Charts' option from the 'Options' tab in the 'Choose a Security' dialog box. Now when you scroll through them, you will see the Smart Charts and everything is back to normal.

From going through this chapter, you will hopefully have seen the value or benefit of using Favorites to group and view your charts—and also, how easy it is to apply different templates and view the same charts in a different way (as we saw using the Guppy MMA template).

8

Custom Buttons –
Just What the
Customer Ordered

 IN A NUTSHELL we will cover:

The use of the Custom Toolbar.

How to create a button.

How to apply a template.

How to open a layout.

How to open a chart.

Things to make MetaStock charting life even easier!

A feature-rich program like MetaStock is bound to have little hidden gems in it to make our lives easier. This one I guess is not really all that hidden, but it is a relatively new feature, it is a gem, and again shows that the developers are 'on the ball'!

What the Custom Toolbar is

The Custom Toolbar is like all the other toolbars, it can be docked somewhere on the screen or it can be a floating toolbar. How you use it is totally up to you, after all, it is a 'custom' toolbar. Here are some of the things we can do with it:

➤ Apply templates.

➤ Open layouts.

➤ Open Charts (although, strangely enough, not Smart Charts).

➤ Launch other programs.

The first three items make perfect sense even to me; the last one I'm not so sure about. By default, i.e. when you load MetaStock, the Custom Toolbar has buttons preconfigured to open your browser and take you to the Equis website. Now whilst this is a nice thought, I find that if I am going to surf the net, it won't be from clicking a button in MetaStock. Of course this feature can be quite useful if you monitor something like cnnfn.com in a window within MetaStock next to a chart.

You may feel differently, in fact some people may find it helpful to have that sort of button in MetaStock, I guess that's where the 'custom' tag comes in. In short, the most practical uses for the Custom Toolbar to me are all directly MetaStock-related—you will find out what works best for you.

We'll step through the process to add the following buttons:

➤ Apply the Guppy MMA Template.

➤ Open the Alan Hull Index Overview Layout.

➤ Open a Chart of IBM.

➤ Apply the Alan Hull Range Indicator template we created earlier (based on the indicators we built).

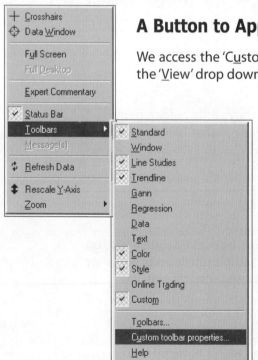

A Button to Apply the Guppy MMA Template

We access the 'Custom toolbar properties…' by selecting 'Toolbars' on the 'View' drop down menu.

This brings up the 'Custom Toolbar Properties' box. My sample box on the opposite page is blank because I deleted all the buttons from it.

We click on the 'New…' button and then use the 'Browse…' button to find the file we need. In this case we are looking for the Guppy MMA template. Navigate through the directories in the usual Windows manner and make sure you have 'Files of type:' set to 'Templates', otherwise you won't be able to see the available template files.

Once you have found the template—'Daryl Guppy MMA.mwt'—select it by clicking on it (it will now be highlighted) and then click on the

'Open' button. This puts the path to the file in the text box, now click the 'Next>' button. Pick an appropriate icon and type in something for the screen tip—this is what shows up when you hover the mouse over a button. It's a good idea to make this something meaningful, you'd be surprised how easy it is to set up a button and then in a few months time forget what it did! Again, click the 'Next>' button—nearly done now—enter text for the Status Bar (see the screen layout diagram in Chapter 1 to locate the Status Bar), something useful, similar to the screen tip, then click on the 'Finish' button.

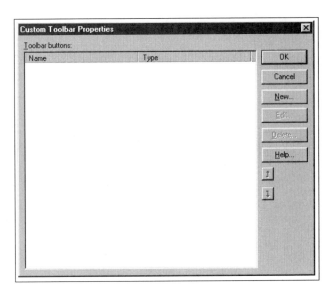

We are now back to the 'Custom Toolbar Properties' box, complete with our new button. If you have deleted all the other buttons in your 'Custom Toolbar Properties' box, then it will look like this:

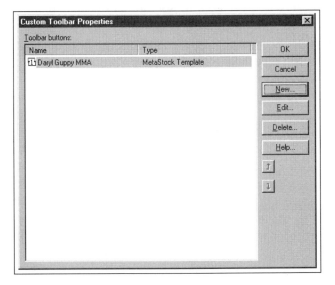

To delete a button (at any time), click on it to select it (so it is highlighted), then simply hit the 'Delete…' button. If nothing is selected, the 'Delete…' button will not be active (it will be grayed out).

Click 'OK' to close the box.

Hmmm… a funny thing may have happened. If you have a Chart or Smart Chart open, then you will now see the icon you picked in the Custom Toolbar (test it out by moving the mouse pointer over it and checking the screen tip). On the other hand, if you have/had no Charts or Smart Charts open, then the button on the Custom Toolbar probably disappeared (especially if this is the only button on the toolbar)!

Don't panic! This is yet another smart feature of the software. I guess it kind of stops you wanting to press buttons that won't do anything. After all, we have created a button to apply a template, not much use trying to click on it if we don't have any charts open! Best to hide it from us, which is exactly what MetaStock does. Open a chart and close it again to see the buttons on the Custom Toolbar appear and disappear (make sure the Custom Toolbar is selected on the Toolbar list—otherwise you'll never see it—remember it should have a 'check mark' next to it in the 'Toolbars' list in the 'View' drop down menu).

Hopefully when you open a chart and click the button, as if by magic, the Guppy MMA indicator appears on a new chart. Now that's certainly easier than going to look for the template each time you want to apply it.

A Button to Open the Alan Hull Index Overview Layout

We are going to go through a similar process to add another button, this time to open a layout.

Bring up the Custom Toolbar Properties box and select 'New…'. When we browse this time, we are looking for 'Files of type:', 'Layouts'. Find the Alan Hull Index Layout we created earlier and click the 'Open' button. Follow the same steps we did for the previous example, enter the screen tip and status bar text, pick an appropriate icon and then click the 'Finish' button.

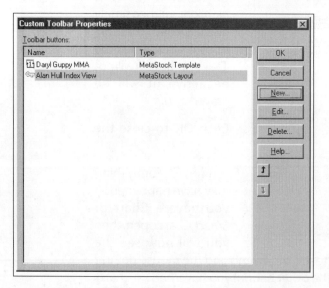

The choice of icons of course is up to you—I picked the yellow 'key'.

Click 'OK' and see what happens. If you had a chart open, then you will see the Custom Toolbar with both buttons—no charts open, then you will see no buttons… but wait… there is a button there! Yes in fact for me, the little yellow key is showing up. There is a good reason for this too. To open a layout, we don't need anything on the screen. It is not like a template that has to be applied to a chart, it doesn't need anything, so MetaStock makes the button available to us, even when the screen is empty.

Click the button and you should see the Alan Hull index View Layout open up (see the example opposite).

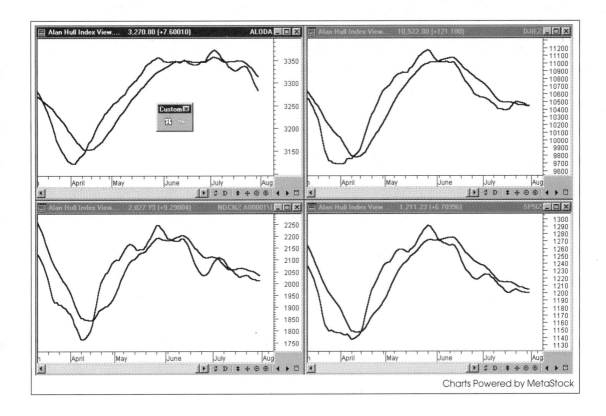

Charts Powered by MetaStock

I floated the Custom Toolbar over the charts so you could see what it looks like. The Daryl Guppy MMA Template button is now visible because we have charts that we can apply templates to.

Alan Hull Range Indicator Button

Well, first we built the Indicator—the Central Cord, the Upper Deviation and the Lower Deviation, then we made it into a Template, now it's time to attach the Template to a button on the Custom Toolbar.

If you haven't quite got a handle on this, I'll step through it, albeit briefly! We will follow the same process we used to create the button that applied the Guppy MMA, except this time the template we will be applying is the Alan Hull Range Indicator template.

Step One: Open the 'Custom Toolbar Properties' box (from menu option 'Custom toolbar properties…') on the 'Toolbars' menu from the 'View' drop down menu.

Step Two:	Select the 'New...' button to create a new button.
Step Three:	Browse the files to find the Alan Hull Range Indicator template – make sure you are looking for 'Files of type:', 'Templates'.
Step Four:	Select an icon, enter a screen tip and status bar text.
Step Five:	Finish!

You will now have a button on the Custom Toolbar menu that applies a template based on the indicators you built...well done!

A Button to Open a Chart of IBM

I think you can probably work this one out for yourself. But just in case, I'll give you the basic steps.

One important thing to start off with is that you must have a saved Chart of IBM (or some other security) and you must know where to find it too.

Select 'New...' from the Custom Toolbar Properties box and then browse for the chart (this time we are looking for 'Files of type:', 'Charts').

Step through the process, entering the appropriate text, and then pick an icon. Finished!

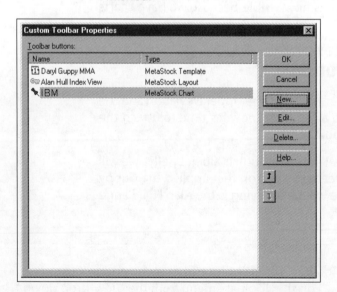

You now have at least three icons on your Custom Toolbar. These are the ones we have created.

When you click 'OK', you will either see all the buttons (if you have charts open) or just the Layout and Chart buttons (that don't require charts already open in order to be displayed).

Click your 'Chart' icon to open the IBM chart (or whatever chart you selected). Hopefully everything has worked and you can now even use the Template button to apply the Guppy MMA template to the chart.

9

The Explorer –
Boldly Going Where
None Have Gone Before

 IN A NUTSHELL we will cover:

What the Explorer is.

A very simple example.

The use of the Filter.

A few of the options available — including setting the periodicity for the Exploration.

Some basic Explorations to try.

How to set up lists.

Seek using binoculars and you will find… or something like that.

The Explorer tool is used to search for and filter securities that meet certain user-specified criteria. In this chapter, we are going to cover enough of the Explorer to get you going. Right, let's get straight into it!

What the Explorer Really Is

The Explorer is a versatile and complex tool. It allows us to search through thousands of securities to find the ones that we really want to look at. We can sift through entire markets with the click of a button and a few minutes of computer time, rather then 'eyeballing' charts until our eyes fall out!

Specifically, though, what is the Explorer? Well, it is a tool that can sort and rank securities or indeed only show us the ones that meet specified criteria.

For example, let's say we wanted to find all those securities that have a closing price today that is greater than yesterday's closing price, and maybe even look at the percentage increase. How would we do it? One way would be to open every chart and see which ones had a higher closing price for today and do a calculation manually. This could take quite some time, especially if you want to examine the entire market! Fear not, because that is what the Explorer can do with ease.

As another example, let's say you had a 'List' of stocks in your portfolio (or a watch list) and you wanted to see what the Moving Average was doing, as well as the closing price. Again you could do it manually by checking the charts, or you could let the Explorer do it for you. Whilst these are both very simple examples, they will hopefully give you an idea as to what this tool can do.

The uses of the Explorer are more or less only limited by your imagination. Just about anything you can think of that involves the Open, High, Low, Close or Volume of a security and any of the Indicators, can most likely be programmed into the Explorer.

In keeping with the Indicator Builder we saw earlier, the Explorer is programmed using the MetaStock Formula Language. This gives us the ability to search for securities using an indicator or a combination of indicators, using the functions of the built-in language.

Knowing what it can do and being able to do it are definitely two different things, so let's take a look at the basic Explorer screen and see what it all means.

We can start the Explorer tool by either clicking on the Binoculars on the Standard Toolbar or selecting it from the 'Tools' drop down menu, or even using the keyboard shortcut 'Ctrl + E' (the usual Windows options!).

This brings up the basic 'Explorer' dialog box, which lists all the available Explorations, including those we build ourselves (see the example opposite). You will notice that once you have run an Exploration, the letter 'R' shows up next to it. This means that there is a report for you to look at which will show you the actual results of the Exploration. The report stays there until you delete it or run the Exploration again.

For now, click on either 'New…' or 'Edit…'—well all right, make it the 'New…' button—to bring up the Exploration Editor.

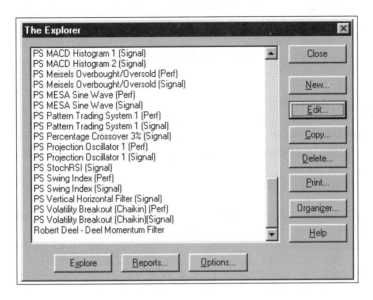

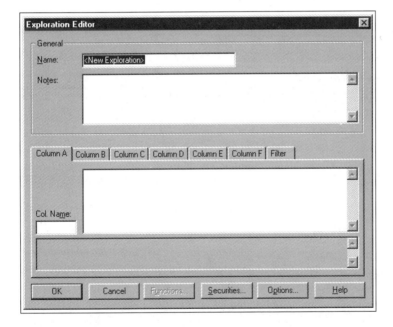

We have six columns, A to F, and a Filter tab. Hmmmm… what do they mean? Well, you can think of the columns as being similar to those of a spreadsheet and the Filter as being, well, a Filter—something that only lets the good stuff go through!

When we run an Exploration and then examine the report, we will see values for each of the columns for each security. For example, Column A might be the closing price, Column B might be the value of the 30-day Simple Moving Average based on the closing price. The report will show the results of what we have requested for each column. An example might make this clearer.

A Basic Exploration

Using the earlier example, say we want to see the closing price and value of the Moving Average (a 30-day Simple Moving Average of the closing price) for a selection of stocks.

In the Exploration Editor, start by entering in a name of the Exploration, 'Close and MA' for example. The 'Notes' section is optional, but like screen tips and descriptions, it can be useful in the future to remind you what the Exploration does.

Now using the MetaStock Formula Language, we are going to enter the code into the required columns. In this case, Column A will show the Closing price, the code for which is just 'C'.

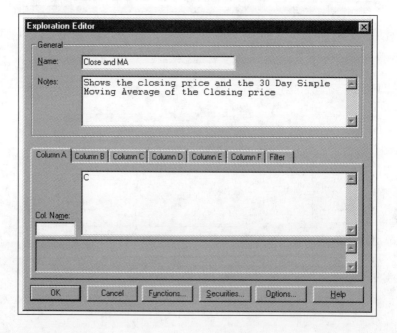

Column B will show the moving average, so we will need to use the 'mov()' function (which we have already used to build an indicator). The code for Column B therefore will be 'mov(C,30,S)'

The 'Col. Name:' is optional, but it can assist in identifying what the columns are on the report!

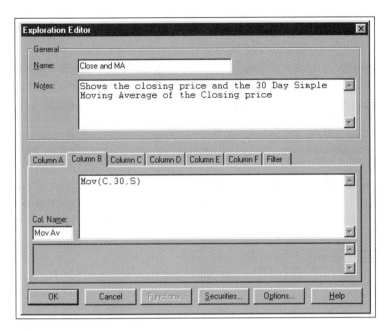

We won't worry about the Filter tab or the Securities and Options buttons for the time being.

Click 'OK' to return to the main Explorer box.

We may as well get right into it now, so click on the 'E**x**plore' button.

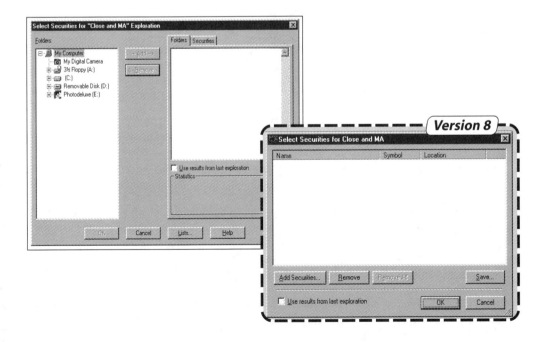

This is where we tell the Explorer what securities we want it to… er… explore! Later on in this chapter we will set up a List, which is a shortcut way to selecting securities.

For now, find your data directory, select a folder and add it to the right-hand box using the '---Add--->' button (note that the Windows shortcut for selecting multiple folders using the Shift and Control keys doesn't work in this section).

Just one folder will do for now. In the 'Statistics' box, you will see how many securities are in the folder and how many will be used in the Exploration. In Version 8, use the 'Add Securities...' button. Select the appropriate securities from the available folders (use 'Tools', 'Select All' to highlight all securities in a folder, or alternatively use the usual Windows shortcuts 'Shift' and 'Ctrl') and click 'Open'. You can continue to add securities in this way until you have selected all the ones you need.

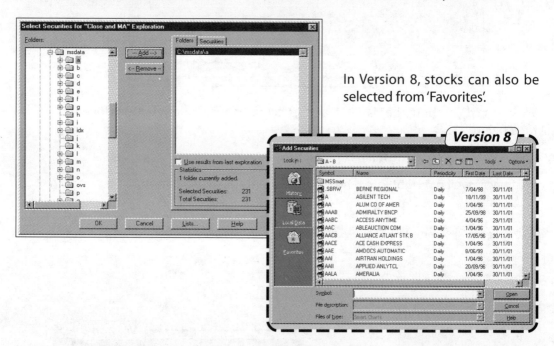

In Version 8, stocks can also be selected from 'Favorites'.

All we have to do now to run this Exploration (in my case on 231 securities) is click the 'OK' button.

The 'Exploration Status' window pops up, giving information about the progress of the Exploration. When it has finished, the 'Exploration Completed' dialog box gives us access to the report—by clicking on the 'Reports…' button..

My report is displayed at the top of the next page.

The report shows us all the securities we selected, the closing price in Column A and the Moving Average (which I renamed Mov Av) in Column B.

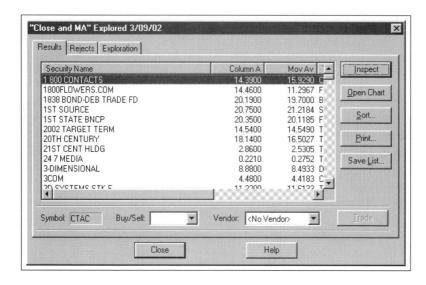

From here we can do any or all of the following:

➤ Sort the results by clicking on the various column headings, e.g. clicking on 'Column A' will sort the results by closing price, from lowest to highest and vice versa (or use the 'Sort...' button).

➤ Inspect the actual values by clicking on the 'Inspect' button.

➤ Highlight one or more charts and view the actual charts by clicking on the 'Open Chart' button.

➤ Save the list of securities for another day, using the 'Save List...' button. (Version 8 saves into 'Favorites' using the 'Add Favorites' dialog box—see page 80.)

➤ 'Print...' the list (I'll leave you to work that one out!).

➤ And last but not least, add selected securities to your Favorites folders. What… there's no button for that… but it can be done… honest! Oh all right, all you have to do is right click on the selected file or files to bring up a handy little shortcut menu with the option 'Add to Favorites…'. The process is the same as what we went through in the chapter on Favorites.

You have now run the Exploration and seen the results. When you return to the main Explorer box, you will notice the 'R' next to the Exploration, indicating that there is a report available for you to view.

You could expand on this basic Exploration by adding things into the other columns like the high price or maybe another Moving Average.

Now you know what you're doing, we'll add in the Filter and see what that does.

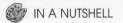

The Filter

The Filter acts just as we would expect a filter to act… it removes what we don't want. In this case, we get to specify what this is, using references to the various Columns and the MetaStock Formula Language.

In the previous example, for instance, we could add in a Filter so the Exploration only shows up those securities that have a closing price above or below a particular dollar amount. To try this out, from the 'Explorer' box highlight the name of the Exploration and click 'Edit…', then add 'colA >10' to the 'Filter' box. Click 'OK' to finish.

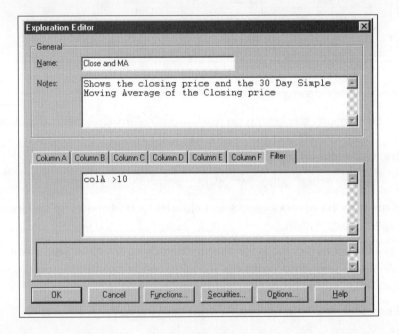

When we run the Exploration now, the Filter will filter out all those securities that have a closing price equal to or less than $10.

With my result, I have clicked on the 'Column A' heading to sort by closing price, from lowest to highest (see the screen shot opposite).

Now the Exploration only shows me the securities with a closing price greater than $10. We could do the same with the Moving Average, or we could even combine the two.

Before we go on and work through some more examples, let's have a look at some Options.

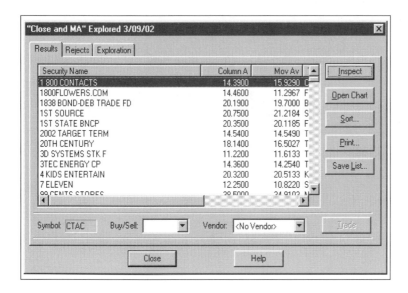

Options!

From the main Explorer box, click on the 'Options...' button.

The only thing we will look at here is the 'Always Prompt for Securities' option. **(This option is not available in Version 8.)** If this is checked, then every time we click the 'Explore' button, the 'Select Securities for….' dialog box comes up. That's OK, from there we simply select the folders we want to explore and away we go, no problems. However, if it is not checked, then each time we run an Exploration, we won't get the option to pick the securities to explore… how strange! In those cases, the Explorer will use the securities we set up for that particular Exploration via the 'Securities…' button in the Exploration Editor. This

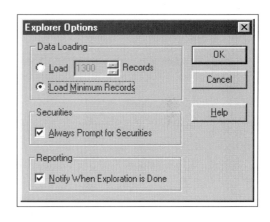

means that for each Exploration we create, we can preset the securities that it will explore. If no securities have been selected anywhere, then the 'Security Selection' box will still come up—it's just that you'll have nothing to explore!

Deselect the option so the check mark is gone (and the box is empty!) and go back to the Editor to see what effect it has.

From the main Explorer box, make sure our sample Exploration is selected and click the 'Edit…' button.

Whilst we're here, a slight detour, click the 'Options…' button first—not to be confused with the 'Options' button in the main 'Exploration' dialog box.

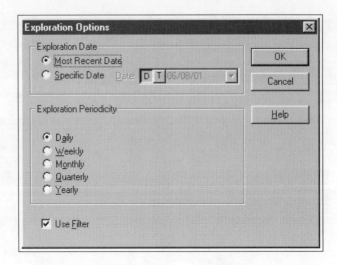

Here is where we can set the periodicity for the Exploration. So if we want to run our Exploration based on weekly data, we would select 'Weekly'—then a 30-day Moving Average would become a 30-week Moving Average and the closing price would be the weekly close. Detour over.

Back to the 'Securities…' button! Click on this button and you will see a very familiar screen.

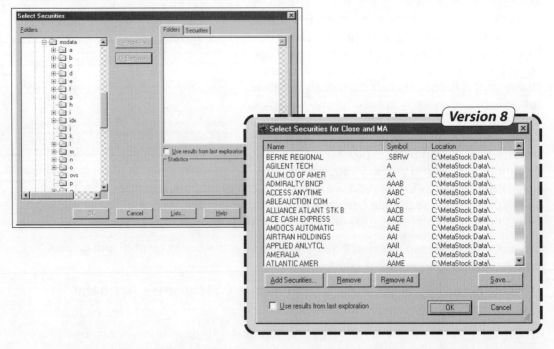

Select the required folders in the usual manner and then click the 'OK' button.

Then click 'OK' again to return to the main Explorer dialog box.

Now when we click 'Explore', the Exploration runs straightaway as it already knows what it has to explore. Please note that in Version 8, it still brings up the 'Selected Securities' dialog box.

How you use this will be up to you. Over time you will sort out the best way to do things. For now I would suggest leaving the check box checked, so that you are always prompted for securities.

Some Examples

As with all the tools in MetaStock, it is worth having a look at the built-in examples to see what can be done. Once you have done that, we can have a look at a few simple practical examples you can create.

Filter on Percentage Increase

Object:	Find all securities where today's closing price is greater than yesterday's closing price plus 20% (i.e. yesterday's close * 1.2).
Column A:	Yesterday's closing price.
Column B:	Today's closing price.
Filter:	Above criteria.

This is going to require the 'ref' function to refer to yesterday's value of the closing price.

Ref(data array,period)

Data array:	The price we are looking at, in this case the closing price – 'close' or 'C'.
Period:	The time we want to look back at (negative) or forward to (positive).

The steps would then be:

Step One:	Open the Explorer.
Step Two:	Create a New Exploration and name it (notes may help too!).

Step Three:	Enter the code as follows:
Column A:	ref(C,-1)
Column B:	C
Filter:	colB > colA*1.2

Note that the MetaStock Formula Language is not case-sensitive. Also, the program will not allow you to enter a formula with incorrect syntax, i.e. not enough parameters.

Run the Explorer and check the results.

Show Percentage Increase

Object:	Show the percentage increase of today's closing price over yesterday's closing price.
Column A:	Yesterday's closing price.
Column B:	Today's closing price.
Column C:	The percentage increase or decrease of today's closing price over yesterday's closing price.

The steps would then be:

Step One:	As for the last example.
Step Two:	As for the last example.
Step Three:	Enter the code as follows:
Column A:	ref(C,-1)
Column B:	C
Column C:	(C/Ref(C,-1)*100)-100

Please note that Column C could also be written using the built-in Rate Of Change function—'roc'.

Roc(data array,period,%or $)

Data array:	The price on which we are doing the rate of change (the closing price).
Period:	The number of periods we are doing it over (one day).
% or $:	Formats the result as either a percentage or as a dollar amount.
Column C:	The alternative Column C formula is: ROC(C , 1, %)

You could use this at the end of each day to rank the securities from those with the greatest increase, down to those that have decreased the most.

Filter for Securities Above a Moving Average

Object:	Find all securities that have a closing price greater than the 30-week Simple Moving Average of the closing price.
Column A:	Today's closing price.
Column B:	The value of the Moving Average.
Filter:	Above criteria.

The steps would then be:

Step One:	As for the last example.
Step Two:	As for the last example.
Step Three:	Enter the code as follows:
Column A:	C
Column B:	mov(C,30,S)
Filter:	colA > colB

Remember to set the 'Options…' in the 'Exploration Editor' to weekly, otherwise the Exploration will work on a 30-day Moving Average.

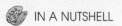

These are all very simple Explorations that hopefully have illustrated what can be done with the Explorer tool. Now you are on your own—equipped with the Help screens, the sky's the limit!

Just before we leave the Explorer tool, we'll have a look and see what these 'Lists' I mentioned are all about.

Lists

The 'Lists…' button is accessed from the 'Select Securities…' box and allows you to set up lists of securities that you can recall at any time for an Exploration. As an example, let's say we were only interested in the top 100 companies by market capitalisation. We could set up a list of these securities and then explore them with different Explorations. Another example would be to set up lists of the different sectors, i.e. one list of all the Energy securities, another for Health Care, etc. This would then allow us to run a particular Exploration on the different sectors, very useful for Relative Strength Comparisons. So a 'List' is just that, a list of securities that we can call up to explore at any time.

To see how this works, open the Explorer, select one of the Explorations (make sure 'Always Prompt for Securities' is checked in the 'Options...') and click the 'Explore' button. From the 'Select Securities…' screen, select a data folder, or use the one already there (if there is one there).

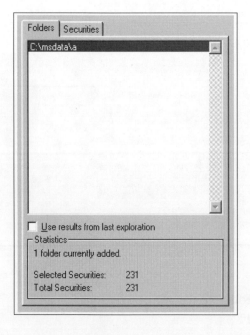

Notice the 'Securities' tab on the right-hand side? If we select it, we can then select and deselect the actual securities within a data folder. In this example (see opposite), instead of having all the securities in the 'a' folder, we can pick, for example, just the blue chip companies.

The tick box at the very top of the list of securities will either select or de-select all the securities in that folder.

Once you have selected a few securities from the folder, click on the 'Lists…' button to bring up the 'Security Lists' box. This shows us all the current lists that we have. We could overwrite an existing list, or create a new one.

To overwrite an existing list, click 'Save As…' and then select the List (to be overwritten) from the list (!). Click on the 'Save' button to overwrite the existing list.

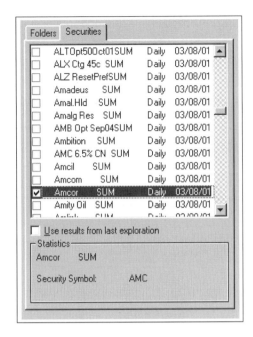

To create a new list, click 'Save <u>A</u>s...' and then enter a new name for the list. Now click on the '<u>S</u>ave' button to save the new list.

To open a list to explore, select a list and click the '<u>O</u>pen' button.

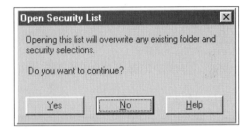

The 'Open Security List' will prompt you to confirm that you want to open that particular list, click the '<u>Y</u>es' button. Your list of folders and securities will now show in the right-hand box, ready for exploring!

Well, that's the end of the 'getting started' introduction to the Explorer tool.

The entire contents of a folder can be selected using the 'Tools', 'Select All' option. Individual or multiple selections can be made by using the Windows selection method—click and CTRL or click and SHIFT.

Note that in Version 8, Lists are added into folders within Favorites. To do this, open an Exploration, add the required securities (using '<u>A</u>dd Securities....' and '<u>O</u>pen') and then select the '<u>S</u>ave...' button to bring up the Add Favorites dialog (as seen on Page 80). Save the list to an appropriate folder or sub-folder in the same way you saved charts into the Favorites folder(s). This folder of securities can then be explored at any time by the Explorer, as can any other folder you have created in Favorites—as long as you select the securities of course! And the reverse also applies; you scroll through the Exploration folders just like normal Favorites folders. Why? Because that's what they are, just normal Favorites folders —how clever!

10

Odds and Ends

 **IN A NUTSHELL** we will cover:

Using an Expert to colour candles.

Two sample screens based on the work of well-known traders.

Something fun to do with the System Tester.

What I haven't told you.

Frequently Asked Questions.

Sometimes there just isn't a heading broad enough!

Well, now we get to the miscellaneous sections, the chapter that covers all the things that don't fit anywhere else. Let's see what we've got left....

Coloring Candles

In MetaStock, the candlestick charts show the candles as black and white by default. The Up candles, where the close is greater than the open, are colored white and the Down candles, where the close is less than or equal to the open, are colored black.

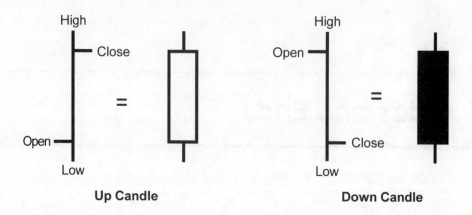

Up Candle   **Down Candle**

Now, whilst this is quite acceptable, there is also a general pseudo 'standard' that has Up days as green and Down days as red. Louise Bedford, author of *The Secret of Candlestick Charting* (and see www.tradingsecrets.com.au), is one such person who much prefers some color in her charts and the thousands of people who have attended her candlestick seminars usually agree.

Well in MetaStock there is some color selection available through the 'Price Plot Properties' box, but the color relationship is based solely on the closing price, i.e. the Up and Down color selections apply to the closing price only, from one period to the next. So for example, if you set the colors as green for Up and red for Down, you might be surprised at the result. (Don't worry, keep reading, all will be revealed!)

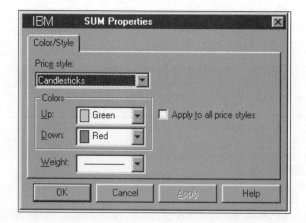

You actually end up with *four* different types of candles—and you only wanted *two!*

These are the possibilities:

An open green candle: The close is above the open and the close today is higher than yesterday's close.

An open red candle: The close is above the open but the close today is lower than yesterday's close.

A solid green candle: The close is below the open but the close today is above yesterday's close.

A solid red candle: The close is below the open and the close today is below yesterday's close.

So in this case:

The candle is coloured red or green depending on the relationship of today's close with yesterday's close. If the close is higher, then the candle is green; if the close is lower, then the candle is red.

The candle is solid if the close is below the open and open (unfilled) if the close is above the open.

All clear? Well I hope so!

Anyway, this is different to the way we really want our candlesticks colored. Normally, we only want to know if the close is above or below the open.

Well, the good news is that there is a way to get MetaStock to emulate this much sought-after color scheme using the 'Expert Advisor'. We won't be going into any detail about the Experts, except to give you a step-by-step guide to program this candlestick chart coloring example.

Click on the Expert Advisor icon (the little man who looks like Charlie Chaplin!).

Or select the 'Expert Advisor…' from the 'Tools' drop down menu.

You are now at the main 'Expert Advisor' window.

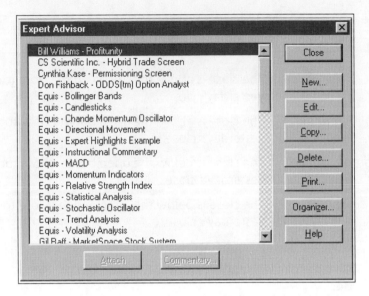

To create our new expert, click the 'New…' button.

This brings up the Expert Editor. Here you can give the Expert a name, something like 'Candlestick Colors' and also add some comments so you know what it does. Like this:

Now select the 'Highlights' Tab. Select 'New' to create a new highlight. Complete the details as per the following:

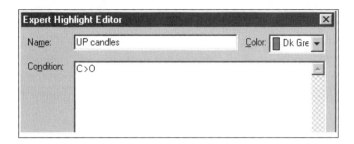

You can use whatever color you want—I selected dark green. Please note that the O is not a zero but an 'O' as in 'Open'! Click 'OK'. You are now ready to enter the second highlight (for down candles—the unhappy ones!).

Click 'New' and complete the second highlight as follows; again, you can use any color you like:

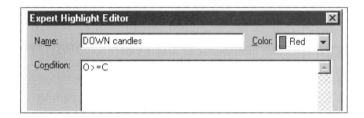

Please note that the O is again an 'O' as in 'Open'!

To finish again, click 'OK'. You should now have something that looks like this:

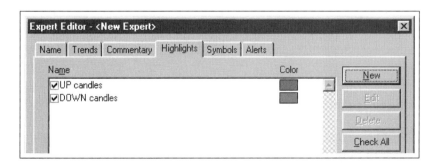

Click 'OK' to return to the main Expert Advisor window.

Create a new chart or open an existing Chart or Smart Chart. Right click on the main chart window to bring up the right click shortcut menu. From here select 'Expert Advisor' and then 'Attach…'. This brings up the 'Attach Expert' box—select the candle coloring expert or whatever you called the Expert and click the 'OK' button.

Your chart will then be colored, with green bars or open candles for when the close is above the open and red bars or solid candles for when the close is below the open—make sure your chart is set to the candlestick variety to get the best effect.

If you attach the Expert to a Smart Chart, then it will be saved with the Smart Chart, so each time you look at it, the candles will be nicely colored. If you attach the Expert to a Chart, you will be prompted to save the changes.

Experts can be included in templates too, so you might create a template that changes a chart to a weekly candlestick chart, colors the candles with the Expert and plots a 30-period Exponential Moving Average (like a chart we will see shortly).

To detach an Expert, right click on the main chart window and select 'Detach' from the 'Expert Advisor' menu.

Two Sample Screens—Based on Well-Known Traders

These sample screens are based on two very well-known Australian traders, who have also written some classic stock market books. For more information see the 'Further Reading' section in Chapter 11. Both sample screens would make great templates.

Louise Bedford (www.tradingsecrets.com.au)

To set up a Louise Bedford-type screen, create a new chart and then do the following:

Step One:	Change the price plot to a Candlestick Chart.
Step Two:	Attach the Candlestick Colouring Expert.
Step Three:	Set the periodicity to 'W' for weekly.
Step Four:	Plot a 30-period Exponential Moving Average of the closing price over the price plot (make sure both the Moving Average and the price plot use the same scale).

You could then save this as a template and apply it to any chart you use (maybe even create a button for it on the Custom Toolbar).

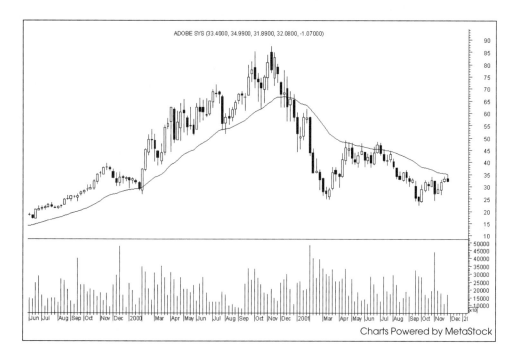

Chris Tate (www.artoftrading.com.au)

This screen setup is from Chris Tate's best-selling *The Art of Trading (2nd Edition)*. A word of caution, Chris uses this purely as an example to illustrate the trading decision. I have included it here to show you how such a screen can be set up in MetaStock, though as Chris says, it is not the 'Holy Grail'!

To set up this style of screen, create a new chart and then do the following:

Step One:	Change the price plot to a Candlestick Chart.
Step Two:	Set the periodicity to 'D' for daily.
Step Three:	Plot an 18-period Weighted Moving Average.
Step Four:	Plot the PS MACD Histogram (now a Custom Indicator in MetaStock) in its own window and change the Style to Histogram, via the 'Color/Style' tab in the 'Indicator Properties' box. Delete the title bar of the inner window.

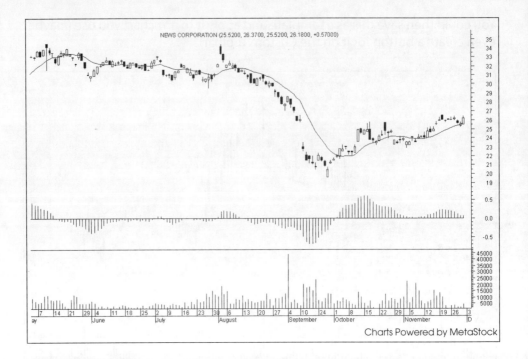

NEWS CORPORATION (25.5200, 26.3700, 25.5200, 26.1800, +0.57000)

Charts Powered by MetaStock

System Tester

This is not something we are going into in any detail, but it's worth having a bit of fun with. Follow these steps:

1. Create a new chart, any chart will do.

2. Start the System Tester tool, either from its icon (the big dollar sign!) or from the 'Tools' drop down menu (or use the keyboard short cut 'Ctrl + T').

3. Select the 'Maximum Profit System' from the list of available System Tests, then click on the 'Test' button.

4. Read the MetaStock Help screen to find out more about this 20/20 hindsight system!

Please note that Version 8 does NOT include this particular system (at time of writing anyway).

What I Haven't Told You!

MetaStock is a very powerful feature-loaded software package. As such, there is no way I could cover all of these features in one book. There are many things I haven't told you, some because I don't use them often, others due to their complexity. It's worth bearing in mind that should you require more tools, the software you bought has probably got them, you just might have to go looking for them.

Here's my list of some of the things I know I didn't cover, that maybe you wished I had:

➤   Fibonacci Retracements.

➤   Gann Lines, Fans and Grids.

➤   How to make money.

➤   The only way to do things—there are other ways to do what's shown in this book, it's just that these work well!

➤   The Data Window.

➤   Crosshairs.

➤   How to make money!!

➤   The Optionscope.

And the list goes on!!

Anyway, before we close another chapter, here is a list of Frequently Asked Questions… and Answers.

Frequently Asked Questions

1.   *I've got the History Disk supplied by my data provider with 15 years worth of information on it—why can't I see all my data?*

Well, the reason that not all the data is showing is probably due to the Load Options. By default, MetaStock only loads in 500 periods, which equates to about two years worth of data. To fix this, increase the number of periods in the 'Load Options…', which is in the 'Options' drop down menu in either the 'New' or 'Open' Chart dialog box.

2.   *Where is my data? It's not here!*

You have to tell MetaStock where your data is. This may mean a bit of navigating around the hard drive to find it, although your data supplier will usually supply you with something that tells you where it will be installed. Check with your supplier if all else fails!

3.   *I've lost the price plot, where's it gone?*

Chances are you have deleted the price plot—somehow! Not to worry, just right click in the main chart window and select 'Display Base Security'. This will re-plot it. Alternatively, you can close the chart down and create another one.

4.   *I've lost volume somehow, how do I get it back?*

Volume is plotted from the Indicator QuickList, so drag it down and plot it. As with the last question, you can always close the chart down and create another one if necessary.

5.   *The Moving Average crosses the price plot at a different point when I zoom in and out, why?*

This can happen when the price and Moving Average are plotted on different scales—they zoom in and out at different rates, hence the crossover points can change. To fix this, right click on the Indicator and select the 'Scaling…'. Make sure it's plotted on the same axis as the price. When it is, you can zoom in and out to your heart's content and the indicator and price will *always* cross at exactly the same spot.

6.   *I think I lost a chart, where is it?*

Have a look in the 'Window' drop down menu—this will list all the open charts. If it is not there, then it probably is really lost, so create a new one!

7.   *Where is XYZ?*

If you can't find a security, then try the 'Find Local Security…' option in the 'Tools' drop down menu of the Chart 'New' or Chart 'Open' dialog box. This can search all data folders and is useful for finding securities that may have changed their names but are still in the original data folder (that is, if your data is separated into alphabetical folders).

8.   *How do I scroll the charts in my Favorites folder without using the mouse?*

The keyboard shortcut for this is 'Alt + →', or 'Alt + ←', where the arrows represent the Cursor control arrows.

9.   *How do I scroll the chart one day at a time?*

Hold down the 'Shift' key and click on the arrow on the chart's Horizontal Scroll Bar. This will move the chart (in either direction) by one period, i.e. one day for a daily chart, a week for a weekly chart, etc.

10.   *Can I have more than one chart on the screen at any one time? If so, how do I see them?*

You can have as many as you want! To see them all, click on 'Tile' in the 'Window' drop down menu.

11.   *How come I'm not making any money then?*

See the 'Further Reading' section (in Chapter 11)!

12. *Why is the 'PS MACD Histogram' indicator showing up as a line?*

    By default, MetaStock plots all indicators as line plots. To see this as a histogram, double click on the indicator and select 'Histogram' from the 'Style:' drop down menu. You could then save this as a template, to save you having to change the style each time you plot it—simply apply the template instead.

13. *I launched MetaStock and it asked for a disk… which one do I put in the computer and why?*

    Newer versions of MetaStock have some 'built in' copy protection. This means that every now and then you will be asked for the original MetaStock program disk… this is the one that contains the actual MetaStock program. Simply insert the disk into your CD drive, click 'OK' and the computer does the rest.

11

Further Reading and Stuff!

 **IN A NUTSHELL** we will cover:

> Must-read books.
>
> Internet sites to check out.
>
> Miscellaneous.

OK, I now know how to use the basics of MetaStock… but I want more… I want to know how to make money!!

Well, I said from the start this book would not tell you how to make money, but I guess in some ways it does. After all, the resources listed in this section will hopefully give you the knowledge required to put your MetaStock charting package to good and profitable use.

Must-Read Books

These are listed by title and author… and are in no particular order!

The Art of Trading – Chris Tate, Wrightbooks.

Understanding Options Trading in Australia – Chris Tate, Wrightbooks.

Taming the Bear – Chris Tate, Wrightbooks.

Share Trading – Daryl Guppy, Wrightbooks.

Trading Tactics – Daryl Guppy, Wrightbooks.

Chart Trading – Daryl Guppy, Wrightbooks.

Better Trading – Daryl Guppy, Wrightbooks.

Snapshot Trading – Daryl Guppy, Wrightbooks.

Trading Secrets – Louise Bedford, Wrightbooks.

The Secret of Candlestick Charting – Louise Bedford, Wrightbooks.

The Secret of Writing Options – Louise Bedford, Wrightbooks.

Let the Trade Wins Flow – Dr Harry Stanton, self – published.

The Success Factor – Dr Harry Stanton, self – published.

Charting in a Nutshell – Alan Hull, Wrightbooks.

Active Investing – A Complete Answer – Alan Hull, Wrightbooks.

Trading with a Plan – Tony Compton and Eric Kendall, Wrightbooks.

Trading on the Australian Stock Market – A Beginner's Guide – Clifton Thornton, Wrightbooks.

Making Money the Smart Way – Jimmy B. Prince, McGraw Hill.

Secret of Profiting in Bull and Bear Markets – Stan Weinstein, McGraw Hill.

Trading for a Living – Dr Alexander Elder, John Wiley & Sons, Ltd.

Trade Your Way to Financial Freedom – Van K. Tharp, McGraw Hill.

Introduction to Technical Analysis – Martin Pring, McGraw Hill.

Technical Analysis Explained – Martin Pring, McGraw Hill.

Technical Analysis of Stock Trends – Edwards and Magee, McGraw Hill.

Technical Analysis of Financial Markets – John Murphy, Prentice Hall.

Market Wizards – Jack Schwager, Harper Collins.

New Market Wizards – Jack Schwager, Harper Collins.

Technical Analysis from A–Z – Stephen Achelis, McGraw Hill.

Richest Man in Babylon – George S. Clason, Penguin.

Think and Grow Rich – Napoleon Hill, Harper Collins.

Investor's Quotient – Jake Bernstein, John Wiley & Sons, Ltd.

The Disciplined Trader – Mark Douglas, Prentice Hall.

Computer Analysis of the Futures Market – Le Beau and Lucas, McGraw Hill.

New Concepts in Technical Trading Systems – J. Welles Wilder, Hunter Publishing.

Reminiscences of a Stock Operator – Edwin Lefevre, John Wiley & Sons, Ltd.

Japanese Candlestick Charting Techniques – Steve Nison, Prentice Hall.

Trader Vic – Methods of a Wall Street Master – Victor Sperandeo, John Wiley & Sons, Ltd.

How I made $2,000,000 in the Stock Market – Nicolas Darvas, Lyle Stuart Inc.

Technical Analysis for the Trading Professional – Constance Brown, McGraw Hill

Fibonacci Ratios with Pattern Recognition – Larry Pesavento, Traders Press Inc.

Beyond Technical Analysis – Tushar S. Chande, John Wiley & Sons.

How to Trade in Stocks – Jesse Livermore, Traders Press Inc.

If it's raining in Brazil, buy Starbucks – Peter Navarro, McGraw Hill.

Liar's Poker – Michael Lewis, Hodder / Coronet.

Pit Bull – Martin 'Buzzy' Schwartz, Harper Business.

The Strategic Electronic Day Trader – Robert Deel, John Wiley & Sons.

The Day Trader From the Pit to the PC – Lewis J. Borsellino, John Wiley & Sons.

Playing for Keeps in Stocks and Futures – Tom Bierovic, John Wiley & Sons.

The Technicians Guide to Day Trading – Martin Pring, Wrightbooks.

New Trading Dimensions – Bill Williams, John Wiley & Sons.

Trading with DiNapoli Levels – Joe DiNapoli.

Computer Analysis of the Futures Markets – LeBeau and Lucas, McGraw Hill.

Schwager on Futures Technical Analysis – Jack Schwager, John Wiley & Sons.

Rocket Science for Traders – John F. Ehlers, John Wiley & Sons.

Antilogic – Bruce McComish, John Wiley & Sons.

Stock Patterns for Day Trading Vol 1 and 2 – Barry Rudd, Traders Press.

The Master Swing Trader – Alan S. Farley, McGraw Hill

The Stock Trader – Tony Oz, Goldman Brown Business Media Inc.

Come into my Trading Room – Dr Alexander Elder, John Wiley & Sons

How I Made One Million Dollars Last Year Trading Commodities – Larry Williams, Windsor

Day Trade Futures Online – Larry Williams, John Wiley & Sons

Rogue Trader – Nick Leeson, Warner

The Predators' Ball – Connie Bruck, Penguin

The Lord of the Rings – J. R. R. Tolkien, Harper Collins (You can't trade all the time!!)

Mindtraps – Roland Barach

Street Smarts – Connors and Raschke

Harry Potter (all of them!) – J. K. Rowling, Bloomsbury

Wrightbooks is an imprint of John Wiley & Sons Australia, Ltd. Books are available from www.wrightbooks.com.au.

Internet Sites to Check Out!

Daryl Guppy – www.guppytraders.com
Louise Bedford – www.tradingsecrets.com.au
Colin Nicholson – www.bwts.com.au
The Educated Investor – www.educatedinvestor.com.au
The Turtle Traders – www.turtletrader.com
Dr Alexander Elder – www.elder.com
Martin Pring – www.pring.com
Equis (the home of MetaStock) – www.equis.com
MetaStock – www.metastock.com
Neil Costa – www.marketmasters.com.au
Traders Press – www.traderspress.com
Traders Library – www.traderslibrary.com
Garnett Znidaric – www.tradingplan.com.au
Guy Bower – www.guybower.com
Nick Katiforis – www.nickkatiforis.com
Alan S. Farley – www.hardrightedge.com
Linda Bradford Raschke – www.lbrcapital.com
Lewis Borsellino – www.teachtrade.com
Robert Deel – www.tradingschool.com
Futuresource – www.futuresource.com
Chicago Board of Trade – www.cbot.com
Chicago Board Options Exchange – www.cboe.com
New York Stock Exchange – www.nyse.com
Chicago Mercantile Exchange – www.cme.com
Dow Jones – www.dowjones.com
Rick LaPoint – www.parttimetrader.com
CNN Financial News – www.cnnfn.com
Tony Oz – www.tonyoz.com
Bill Williams – www.profitunity.com
Joe DiNapoli – www.fibtrader.com
Stocks and Commodities – www.traders.com
Active Trader Magazine – www.activetradermag.com
Tom Bierovic – www.synergytrader.com
Investors Edge – www.investorsedge.com.au
John Murphy/Greg Morris – www.murphymorris.com
Jon DeBry – www.debry.com
Lincoln Indicators – www.lincolnind.com.au
Australian Technical Analysts Association – www.ataa.com.au

Index

To Subscribe to a FREE monthly MetaStock E-Tips Newsletter

Email:

MetaShell@bigpond.com

Or write to:

Simon Sherwood
PO Box 97
Highett
Victoria
Australia   3190

(Make sure you include your email address!)

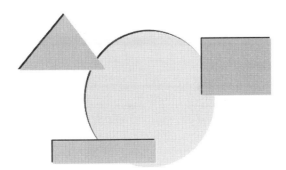

You'll also be kept up to date about:

➤ Upcoming MetaStock training courses

➤ Future publications (like the possible 'Advanced MetaStock® in a Nutshell'!)

➤ Technical Analysis using MetaStock.

You should also have a look at the Yahoo MetaStock group, to share your tips and tricks or have your questions answered:

http://au.groups.yahoo.com/group/metashell